# THE HOMEWORK CONUNDRUM

Homework has a key role to play in strengthening memory, building attainment and helping students to develop transferable, life-long study skills. If done right, regular, good-quality homework has the potential to bridge achievement gaps and help all students become successful, confident learners.

Rooted in robust cognitive science principles, this book provides a clear guide for how a successful homework culture can be built in a school and within the classroom. With a focus on making homework an integral part of teaching and learning, it includes practical strategies on how to get students, staff and parents to value the homework that is set, ensuring it is built into sustainable practice, so all parties can reap its many benefits. Chapters cover:

- Cognitive science principles and homework

- The features of effective homework

- Parental role and involvement

- Supporting all students

- Rewards and sanctions

- Motivation and attainment

Part of The InnerDrive Teacher CPD Academy series that offers a deep dive into the key areas that matter to teachers, this book is essential reading for all teachers and leaders wanting to ensure that homework is well designed, evidence-informed, implemented consistently and valued by all members of the school community.

**Jovita M. Castelino** is the curriculum leader for science at Trinity Academy Cathedral, Wakefield. She is an experienced teacher with a special interest in applying cognitive science principles to teaching to maximise student learning.

**The Teacher CPD Academy**
Series editors: Bradley Busch and Edward Watson

# THE HOMEWORK CONUNDRUM

## How to Stop the Dog From Eating Homework

Jovita M. Castelino

Routledge
Taylor & Francis Group

LONDON AND NEW YORK

Designed cover image: InnerDrive

First published 2025
by Routledge
4 Park Square, Milton Park, Abingdon, Oxon OX14 4RN

and by Routledge
605 Third Avenue, New York, NY 10158

*Routledge is an imprint of the Taylor & Francis Group, an informa business*

*British Library Cataloguing-in-Publication Data*
A catalogue record for this book is available from the British Library

ISBN: 978-1-032-56332-9 (hbk)
ISBN: 978-1-032-56333-6 (pbk)
ISBN: 978-1-003-43498-6 (ebk)

DOI: 10.4324/9781003434986

Typeset in Interstate
by KnowledgeWorks Global Ltd.

# CONTENTS

# ACKNOWLEDGEMENTS

It all started during lockdown. I had time on my hands, it was nearly the Summer and I had things to say. But I also finally had the confidence to say them and so I wrote a post and shared it on Twitter (as it was called back then).

Adam Boxer shared that post and suddenly people were reading what I was writing. Teacher Tapp kindly featured some of my posts as their Daily Reads and my writing got even more noticed. I joined the CogSciSci community and learnt much from them, particularly Adam Boxer, Adam Robbins, Niki Kaiser and Pritesh Raichura. They have all been incredibly supportive of me.

My brilliant friends, Claudia Allan and Tom Millichamp, supported me massively. Not just in terms of my thinking but also emotionally, when I felt down.

The leadership team at Cardinal Heenan Catholic High School gave me an amazing opportunity – to lead on homework school-wide. Working with Lizzie Stockton-Pitt, Alice Thomas, Dominic Kelly, Janette Whitelaw, Charlotte Felton, Lauren Burns, Lianne Hudson, Rory O'Flanagan, Sonia Crossland, Daniel Fletcher and many others helped me develop a sensible approach to homework. They not only encouraged me but also challenged me when needed.

Then researchED London, 2022, happened. It was the second time I had applied to present and this time I chose to speak about homework.

At the end of my talk, my throat parched from speaking (and making several excellent jokes), Bradley Busch approached to thank me. Needless to say, I was in shock. I had already read *The Science of Learning* and used a couple of the pages in my work on homework at my school. Brad introduced me to his publisher, Annamarie Kino at Routledge, and the next thing I knew, I was writing a book on homework! Many thanks to both for giving me a chance. Thank you also to the whole editing team, Edward Watson, Patrick Ibbotson, Sameea Begum and Jenien Kawwa for their advice, support and chats. The diagrams in this book look amazing because of the hard work of Lou Bogatchek to whom I am very grateful!

There is one person who has had my back and always given me her time, even it meant a phone call whilst travelling home. I am forever indebted to Ruth Ashbee – a brilliant, witty, exceptional human being.

I am grateful to my current school, Trinity Academy Cathedral, particularly Anna Gillinder, Jennifer Webb, Ruth Lawson, Stephanie Dearnley, Olivia Gorst, Gerry-Lee Pierre, William Thackray and Nichola Leech for their encouragement.

Special thanks also to Jo Davies, Sarah Henderson, Kathryn Evans, Donna Arding, Vikki Furness, Mel Pearce, Ali Griffin and Jude Runnalls for their support and love when I first started teaching.

The writing process has been hard. I have spent many evenings, weekends and holidays researching and writing and none of it would have been possible if I didn't have the support and encouragement of my loving parents and sister, my brilliant husband, Matt, and my two amazing kids, Noah and Zara. They are my life and I hope they are proud of me.

# FOREWORD

I am immensely proud to be writing the foreword to *The Homework Conundrum*. It is the first in our 'Teacher CPD Academy' series and I couldn't think of a better book, on such an important topic, to do so.

Despite being a mainstay in the educational lives of students, so many questions around homework keep popping up. How much impact does it actually have? Is it about quantity or consistency? What roles should parents play in it? Fortunately for all of us, Jo has read the research and skilfully and critically pieced it all together to provide some much-needed clarity.

As well as covering the latest and greatest research, which ranges from large-scale reviews to seminal cognitive science theories, there is a wealth of personal and practical advice. This makes the research not only interesting but crucially, useful.

Homework is perhaps one of the most polarising topics of education discourse, yet Jo approaches it with balance, curiosity and nuance. As a result, *The Homework Conundrum* is both enlightening and pragmatically useful. By the time you turn the final page, you will be one step nearer to really making homework work.

As with all books in this series, we have an accompanying module on this topic on our online platform www.teachercpdacademy.com. Along with Jo's training on homework, you can find a range of topics on teaching and learning, which include self-access modules, interviews with researchers and lesson materials.

We hope that this book, and the whole series, illuminates key research, inspires reflection and sparks discussions. If it does that, then ultimately it will improve and enrich the lives of your students.

Bradley Busch and Edward Watson, Directors of InnerDrive.

# Introduction

Homework has the power to elevate learning.

There is a wealth of research and experience that tells us that learning is an ongoing process. Regular, good-quality homework can help students build confidence, strengthen their memory, achieve better and develop transferable study habits.

I didn't always think about homework in this way.

Let me share a glimpse of my past, of my views on homework before a shift in my thinking took shape.

Picture this: after a long day at school, battling both the sweltering 50°C temperatures (I grew up in Kuwait) and the demands of learning, I would return home, utterly exhausted. But there was one small yet significant saviour that never failed to welcome me - a wave of cool, refreshing breeze from the air conditioner, embracing me as I stepped through the door. Ah, the comfort of collapsing onto the sofa, yearning for a blissful nap, only to be reminded of the looming homework that awaited me. Homework that entailed pages and pages of practice, most of which wasn't even checked by the teacher.

Sometimes, I reluctantly dragged myself to the dining table, facing an overwhelming pile of tasks. Other times, the rebel inside me

DOI: 10.4324/9781003434986-1

took charge, tempting me to indulge in TV shows instead of doing my homework.

As the years passed and I became a teacher myself, I found my perspective was unchanged – I still didn't think much of homework. I encountered a few challenges related to homework:

- Preparing homework tasks for my students took up precious time.

- The process of marking and feeding back on stacks of completed work proved to be quite time-consuming.

- Worst of all, precious class time had to be sacrificed for setting homework instead of using it to teach content.

However, I was setting it because I thought that was what we had to do. In the many years I have been teaching, I did not attend a single Continuing Professional Development (CPD) session or get *any* training on homework. A lot of the focus on training was on what we did in the classroom. And yet, teachers in many schools around the world are expected to set homework and use the data in part to inform student attitudes to learning.

Teachers are busy individuals who are, rightly, focused on improving student achievement and confidence in the classroom. Amidst all the jobs teachers have to do, we have to plan excellent lessons, mark assessments, provide feedback often, monitor student attainment data, manage behaviour in the classroom and communicate with parents. As a result, homework is seen by some as either being relatively unimportant, unnecessary or as something that actively harms students.

In recent times, there has been a shift in our thinking and application of how we learn. This change has revolutionised my teaching so much that my lessons during the early parts of my teaching career bear no resemblance to the lessons I deliver now.

During the COVID pandemic, when we were setting lots of home learning tasks for students to work through independently, I realised that several of my students struggled with it, partly because I hadn't been training them to be independent learners all along. As we returned to the classroom, I started to develop my thinking around homework and it struck me that we knew so much about the principles of learning but we weren't applying these to independent study.

In *The Homework Conundrum*, I share insights from research, my own experience and what we know about learning to call for a change in perspective on homework. I set out a model for excellent homework that will help students, teachers and parents view learning as something that takes place over time and not as a one-off event in the classroom or at home. I discuss how schools can work together with families to ensure homework is effective, not just in terms of the mechanics of setting and feeding back on it but also in terms of the attitudes and perceptions around it.

It is only then that we can realise the power of effective homework and help our students become proficient learners who are confident and motivated to learn.

# 1  Why Should We Talk About Homework?

Homework tends to divide people.

It certainly has an image problem. Search for images of the term 'homework' on a search engine and you will invariably find the little, innocent faces of children pulling their hair out or with forlorn expressions.

People feel strongly about homework because they perceive it to be:

- busy-work

- encroaching on family time

- as forcing children to work beyond school

In my personal experience, I have certainly set homework that did all of these things; so these perceptions are not untrue, at least not when describing my past practice.

Based on data gathered by Teacher Tapp, a survey app, a majority of teachers set homework (89% of 5849 secondary school teachers that were surveyed).

Why do so many teachers set homework? Does the research support any benefits of homework?

DOI: 10.4324/9781003434986-2

When research on homework is cited, it tends to be the figure quoted by the Homework Toolkit produced by the Education Endowment Foundation (EEF, 2021). The EEF has delved into the research to produce an astonishing value of 5 months of additional progress for students who regularly do their homework at the secondary level (3 months at primary). This means that if students don't do their homework or do it sporadically, they could potentially be 5 months behind their peers. For school leaders, the fact that this is a relatively low-cost intervention and that parents expect their children to do homework makes this an exciting figure.

---

**To Note**

The effect size, first introduced by psychologist Jacob Cohen, is a standardised index that allows researchers to compare the impact of different educational interventions or strategies across studies (Cohen, 1992).

An effect size (or d) of approximately 0.2 is considered to show a small effect. It suggests that the difference between the group receiving the intervention and the one not receiving it is 0.2 standard deviations apart.

An effect size, d, of approximately 0.5 suggests a moderate effect with a standard deviation of 0.5 separating the two groups.

An effect size, d, of 0.8 or more suggests a substantial effect with a standard deviation of 0.8 separating the two groups.

---

However, the EEF does acknowledge that the evidence base is limited. Let's look at the studies included in the Toolkit to see why this is the case (Table 1.1).

As the EEF acknowledges, the 3–5-month figure is an average. Looking at the analysis of the studies included in the Toolkit, particularly as most of the studies focused on homework in mathematics, it is very difficult to extrapolate these findings school-wide.

*Table 1.1* A summary of the studies included in the EEF guidance on homework.

| | Primary | Secondary |
|---|---|---|
| **Number of studies** | 11 | 33 |
| **Range of effect sizes** | 0.020-0.722 | -1.98 to 2.46 |
| **Percentage of studies showing a negative effect size** | 0% | 15% |
| **Range of years of studies** | 1987-2017 | 1972-2019 |
| **Percentage of studies focused on mathematics homework** | 55% | 61% |
| **Comments on studies** | A minority (27%) of the studies looked at the effect of flipped learning homework (tasks whereby students teach themselves new content and apply it when next in the classroom). A few of the studies were dissertations submitted towards either a master's or a doctor of philosophy degree. | The majority (70%) of studies looked at the effect of flipped learning homework. In some cases, the studies focused on the effect of flipped homework versus traditional homework rather than homework versus no homework. Many of the studies were dissertations submitted towards either a master's or a doctor of philosophy degree. |

Before we look further into the research on homework, there are a few things to consider:

## Definition of Homework

Studies often differ in their definitions of homework, duration, frequency and types of tasks given. There is no consensus on any of these attributes of homework, which makes it increasingly difficult to extrapolate findings from one context to another.

## Confounding Variables

Several studies on homework are conducted in classroom settings. Whilst the obvious advantage of these is that they are based on real-life situations, we cannot fully isolate the effects of homework from factors such as parental involvement, teaching quality, access to resources, personal circumstances and student motivation, all of which could influence student outcomes. In fact, with the latter, students who voluntarily complete homework might be highly academically motivated, leading to biased results.

In addition, a number of studies on homework tend to rely on self-reports for either the amount of homework set, how often it is set or the time spent doing homework. These measures will undoubtedly influence the results with students, parents or teachers involved in the research potentially distorting their reports due to inaccuracies in reporting on past events.

## Research by Cooper et al.

Harris Cooper is an American psychologist who has had a significant influence on policy through his extensive research into the benefits and drawbacks of homework. Most notably, he has published reviews of the literature on homework and its impact on student academic achievement.

Cooper's meta-analyses, reviewing 120 studies in 1980 and over 60 studies in 2006, drew three main conclusions (Cooper, 1989, 2006):

- Homework positively influences student academic achievement. The impact is stronger for secondary school students compared to primary students.

- Too much homework is counterproductive. Cooper suggests setting 10 minutes of homework per day for each grade level is most effective. For instance, a student in Year 6 should get 60 minutes of homework.

- Homework is expected to (a) encourage students to learn during their free time, (b) improve students' attitudes towards school and (c) improve students' study habits.

### Conclusion 1: Homework Positively Impacts Academic Achievement

This is the oft-quoted reason for setting homework and one with which parents and teachers generally agree. But is this just an experiential claim or one rooted in evidence?

Fascinatingly, in 1989, Cooper found that the mean effect size of doing homework versus no homework on achievement was 0.21 (Cooper, 1989). In 2006, he found the mean effect size was increased to 0.60 (Cooper, 2006). Cooper et al. attributed this to more robust studies (from a range of sources including journal articles, conference papers and dissertations) as they included comparable control groups, which the initial studies included in 1989 did not.

The Department for Education (DfE) published the results of a large longitudinal study called the Effective Pre-School, Primary and Secondary Education Project (EPPSE). They focused on around 3100 students (over 2700 were studied till they completed the Key Stage 4 level) and looked at various factors affecting attainment. One of these factors was how long was spent on homework at various stages of the students' time in school. The study found that spending any time on homework compared to no homework at all improved student outcomes significantly. By the time students reached Year 11, spending over 3 hours on homework per night was most impactful (Sammons, 2014). It has to be noted that although this is promising, students used self-reports to provide the time they spent on homework. Furthermore, there was no further research into the type or quality of homework set.

A more recent meta-analysis, dating from 2006 to 2015, focused on 11 studies on homework and found an overall modest positive association between homework and attainment (d = 0.229). Delving into the research further, however, reveals that there were larger effect sizes for studies with larger sample sizes (d = 0.498) that were published (d = 0.572) versus dissertations (d = 0.254) and at the secondary-grade equivalent (d = 0.479). None of these differences were statistically significant, although the researchers suggest that various confounding factors and flaws in study design could have influenced results (Baş, 2017).

Finally, Fan et al. analysed the results from 28 studies ranging from 1986 to 2015. These studies found an overall positive relationship between homework and achievement in maths and science. Indeed, they found larger effect sizes for homework completion (d = 0.594), homework performance or grade (d = 0.517) and homework effort (d = 0.307) compared to the frequency of homework (d = 0.117) or the time spent on homework (d = 0.145) (Fan, 2017).

So, what does the research really say? All of the research and meta-analyses suggest a modest positive association between homework and attainment. However, there are a number of confounding factors to consider, in addition to the fact that most of the studies focus on mathematics homework and attainment.

Indeed, in their book on the evidence on homework, Hallam and Rogers conclude that the relationship between homework and attainment is complex and a lot of care needs to be taken to consider the research.

Prior knowledge and attainment, socio-economic background, amount of homework that is set, parental aspirations and teacher feedback are some of the factors influencing the effects of homework (Hallam, 2018).

*Summary:* The issue we have is one of bias. Those of us who advocate for the implementation of homework may only see the modest yet positive impact of homework on student outcomes, particularly in terms of academic achievement. Conversely, those of us who harbour concerns about homework encroaching upon our children's leisure time and exacerbating anxiety may perceive these studies as inconclusive or even negative in their findings.

There are many factors that need to be considered before we can quote any research on homework with confidence. In addition, we have the fact that the majority of studies are based in one region (USA) and on limited subjects (usually mathematics).

The chapters that follow will aim to provide a clear and thoughtful lens with which to view homework, ensuring it has a positive impact on our students whilst not being detrimental to them.

## Conclusion 2: Quantity of Homework Matters (But Does It?)

We've already seen that Cooper et al. have supported the '10-minute' rule whereby students do homework for 10 minutes per day per grade level they belong to (Cooper, 2006).

We've also seen that the EPPSE report suggested that over 3 hours of homework per day was strongly associated with positive outcomes for students in Year 11 (Sammons, 2014). According to the 10-minute homework rule, a student in Year 11 should do around 2 hours of homework per day.

In general, it seems that the more homework assigned to students in secondary school, the better their grades/assessment scores. This was certainly the case with research conducted by Timothy Keith (1982) on over 20,000 students, where it was found that increasing the amount of time spent on homework during the week was associated with increased grades, after accounting for ethnicity, family background and prior attainment.

A study based on surveys from more than 7000 students showed that doing any homework was positively associated with test scores compared to doing no homework at all but after controlling for various factors such as attendance and motivation, this association was no longer significant. Additionally, students who did over 2 hours of homework per night achieved similar scores to those who did less than 30 minutes of homework (Maltese, 2012).

Yet another study focusing on data from the Programme for International Student Assessment (PISA) 2012 student surveys of nearly 5000 students found that a 1 standard deviation increase in time spent on homework was associated with a 0.21 standard deviation increase in mathematics achievement (Cheema, 2015).

*Summary:* Taken together, all of this suggests that there is an optimum time that must be spent on homework for it to be impactful but that too much is detrimental to outcomes. However, Marzano and Pickering warn us to make the distinction between the time spent on homework and the amount of homework that the student actually completes, the latter of which is a far more powerful and impactful measure of the effectiveness of homework on student outcomes (Marzano, 2007). In a similar vein, when Plant et al. looked at the impact of study time on Grade Point Average (GPA) scores, study time was only significantly associated with higher GPA scores when the quality of the study time was taken into consideration (Plant, 2005).

## Conclusion 3: Homework Can Build Good Habits

In her article on homework, Janine Bempechat says: '...developmentally appropriate homework plays a critical role in the formation of positive learning beliefs and behaviours, including a belief in one's academic ability, a deliberative and effortful approach to mastery, and higher expectations and aspirations for one's future' (Bempechat, 2019).

This is a powerful statement and one that teachers all over the world no doubt want to be true of their students. This sentiment is echoed by Redding who says that regular homework develops the habit of self-study and independent learning (Redding, 2000).

In order to be successful at homework and for it to have beneficial effects on attainment, completing homework requires the employment of self-regulated behaviours such as ignoring distractions (Xu, 2022). In fact, it is important to note the behaviours that involve self-regulation. Zimmerman defines them as the process of setting goals, selecting the right learning strategies, managing self-motivation and continually monitoring and evaluating progress (Zimmerman, 2000).

Corno challenges us to look at homework as something that can be gratifying, a path for knowledge to travel from school to home and back and a way to build academic rigour. She warns us not to make home-work enticing as the 'fun' elements could divert attention away from the learning. She goes further to summarise the impact of homework on non-academic outcomes with students feeling less anxious and building their self-esteem over time (Corno, 2000).

Research by Zimmerman et al. found that homework practices pre-dicted students' beliefs over their ability to learn. Interestingly, they also found that good homework practices were only linked to higher attainment if students believed they could learn (Zimmerman, 2005).

*Summary:* There appears to be a cyclical relationship between self-regulatory behaviours and homework practices that lead to higher aca-demic achievement. Students who believe they can learn, achieve well and can ignore distractions tend to gain the most benefit from their homework. The reverse is also true – students who get regular homework can develop self-regulatory behaviours over time (Bembennuty, 2011) (Figure 1.1).

Homework ⇄ Self-regulation

*Figure 1.1* The cyclical relationship between homework and self-regulation.

## Research by Hattie

In his book, *Visible Learning*, John Hattie analysed five meta-analyses on homework, totalling 161 studies. His synthesis of the research delivered an average effect size of 0.29. This suggests a low-moderate impact on student outcomes. The effect sizes range from 0.15 for primary-aged students to 0.64 for secondary-aged students (Hattie, 2008).

One of the reasons provided for the low effect size for homework in primary schools is that younger children may struggle with organising their time or independent study. According to Hallam et al., a survey conducted by the Office for Standards in Education, Children's Services and Skills (Ofsted, a non-ministerial department of the UK government responsible for inspecting and regulating educational institutions and children's social care services) suggested that homework at the primary level was not an integral part of the school curriculum (Hallam, 2018).

Cooper and Hattie assert that if the implementation cost is low, an intervention may still be valuable even if the effect size is small.

Additionally, Hattie reminds us that these meta-analyses focused on homework as it *was* rather than what it could be. Our knowledge of learning has progressed drastically over the past few decades with implications from research effecting changes within the classroom. Setting homework that fosters learning is crucial to enhance its impact on student success.

All the research showing the positive impact of homework on student outcomes (either academic or non-academic) suggests that the following key factors must be considered first:

### *The Teacher's Self-Efficacy*

When the teacher believes that their effort, planning and instructions can positively impact their students' academic achievement, there is a higher chance that they will be successful in doing so (Bembennuty, 2011).

Consider two teachers:

| | Teacher A | Teacher B |
|---|---|---|
| **Planning** | Teacher A sets homework that they find in a shared folder containing centralised resources. | Teacher B carefully plans the learning students must achieve at the end of a sequence. As part of this, they plan the homework that will help students practice retrieval of key content from within the current topic and from previously learnt content. |
| **Setting** | When setting the work, Teacher A tells students what the homework is and when it is due. The homework tends to be on current work studied in the classroom. | When setting the work, Teacher B explicitly tells students how the homework will benefit them and why they have designed it the way they have. |
| **Feedback** | On submission day, Teacher A provides the answers using the mark scheme but when the students contest an answer, they are unable to provide a clear explanation as to why the mark scheme is right or wrong. | On submission day, Teacher B goes through the answers and provides feedback, knowing how each response will either progress learning or provide insight into any misconceptions students hold. |

Teacher B clearly knows the impact their planning will have on student learning. They have a clear idea of what to expect and set up homework in such a way that it achieves the intended goals. This self-efficacy and assuredness come from a place of knowledge of how learning happens and the context-specific aspects of how to get the best of their students. Chapter 2 will discuss the key principles to consider when thinking of homework.

### Purpose and Type of the Homework Task

As in the scenario with Teacher B above, if students understand the purpose of the homework that has been set, they are more likely to buy-in and understand the benefits of the work. In the same vein, certain types of homework are more powerful in eliciting benefits than others (Marzano, 2001) (more on this in Chapter 3).

### Recognition of and Feedback on Homework

Teachers that recognise the effort made into completing homework and provide timely feedback inherently make the homework more effective (Paschal, 1984; Xu, 2008; Cunha, 2018). The type of feedback can have varying impacts on student engagement and outcomes. For instance, if feedback from a teacher is seen as being controlling in nature or punitive, then this can have a negative effect on student motivation (Trautwein, 2006).

### Discussions Over Self-Regulatory Behaviours in the Classroom

Whilst homework is a task that takes place outside of the teacher's influence (away from the classroom), it may seem that there is little a teacher can control in terms of the practices involved.

However, structured discussions and modelling behaviours such as how to monitor one's progress within the classroom can be powerful strategies to employ (Bembennuty, 2011) (more on this in Chapter 3).

## The Student's Motivation and Self-Belief

Whilst homework can influence student motivation and self-belief, it helps if students actually believe they can achieve well if they do their homework properly (Bembennuty, 2011). Homework that is done with minimal effort or by copying the responses from elsewhere, whilst ticking the box for completion, will have no benefit on student outcomes (Trautwein, 2006) (more on this in Chapter 9).

## Chapter Summary

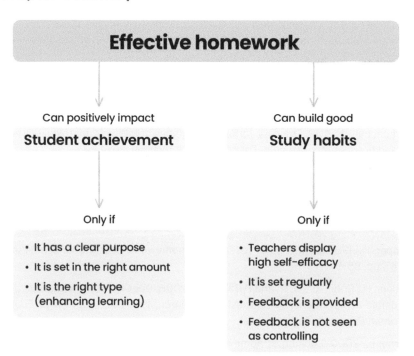

# References

Baş, G., Centürk, C. and Cigerci, F. M., 2017. Homework and academic achievement: A meta-analytic review of research. *Issues in Educational Research*, 27(1), pp. 31–50.

Bembennuty, H., 2011. Meaningful and maladaptive homework practices: The role of self-efficacy and self-regulation. *Journal of Advanced Academics*, 22(3), pp. 448–473.

Bempechat, J., 2019. The case for (quality) homework: Why it improves learning and how parents can help. *Education Next*, 19(1), pp. 36–43.

Cheema, J. R. and Sheridan, K., 2015. Time spent on homework, mathematics anxiety and mathematics achievement: Evidence from a US sample. *Issues in Educational Research*, 25(3), pp. 246–259.

Cohen, J., 1992. A power primer. *Psychological Bulletin*, 112(1), pp. 155–159.

Cooper, H., 1989. Synthesis of research on homework. *Educational Leadership*, 47, pp. 85–91.

Cooper, H., Robinson, J. C. and Patall, E. A., 2006. Does homework improve academic achievement? A synthesis of research, 1987-2003. *Review of Educational Research*, 76(1), pp. 1–62.

Corno, L., 2000. Looking at homework differently. *Elementary School Journal*, 100(5), p. 529.

Cunha, J., Rosário, P., Núñez, J. C., Nunes, A. R., Moreira, T. and Nunes, T., 2018. "Homework feedback is...": Elementary and middle school teachers' conceptions of homework feedback. *Frontiers in Psychology*, 9, pp. 1664–1078.

EEF, 2021. *Homework*. (Online) Available at: https://educationendowment foundation.org.uk/education-evidence/teaching-learning-toolkit/homework#nav-closing-the-disadvantage-gap

Fan, H., Xu, J., Cai, Z., He. J. and Fan, X., 2017. Homework and students' achievement in math and science: A 30-year meta-analysis, 1986-2015. *Educational Research Review*, 20, pp. 35–54.

Hallam, S. and Rogers, L., 2018. *Homework: The Evidence*. 2nd ed. London: UCL Institute of Education Press.

Hattie, J. A. C., 2008. *Visible Learning: A Synthesis of Over 800 Meta-Analyses Relating to Achievement*. Oxford: Routledge.

Keith, T. Z., 1982. Time spent on homework and high school grades: A large-sample path analysis. *Journal of Educational Psychology*, 72(2), pp. 248–253.

Maltese, A. V., Tai, R. H. and Fan, X., 2012. When is homework worth the time? Evaluating the association between homework and achievement in high school science and math. *High School Journal*, 96(1), pp. 52-72.

Marzano, R. J. and Pickering D. J., 2007. The case for and against homework. *Educational Leadership*, 64, pp. 74-79.

Marzano, R. J., Pickering, D. J. and Pollock, J. E., 2001. *Classroom Instruction that Works: Research-Based Strategies for Increasing Student Achievement*. Association for Supervision and Curriculum Development.

Paschal, R. A., Weinstein, T. and Walberg, H. J., 1984. The effects of homework on learning: A quantitative synthesis. *The Journal of Educational Research*, 78(2), pp. 97-104.

Plant, E. A., Ericsson, K. A., Hill, L. and Asberg, K., 2005. Why study time does not predict grade point average across college students: Implications of deliberate practice for academic performance. *Contemporary Educational Psychology*, 30(1), pp. 96-116.

Redding, S., 2000. *Parents and Learning*. International Academy of Education.

Sammons, P., Sylva, K., Melhuish, E., Siraj, I., Taggart, B., Toth, K. and Smees, R., 2014. *Influences on Students' GCSE Attainment and Progress at Age 16. Effective Pre-School, Primary & Secondary Education Project (EPPSE)*. Department for Education.

Trautwein, U., Lüdtke, O., Schnyder I. and Niggli, A., 2006. Predicting homework effort: Support for a domain-specific, multilevel homework model. *Journal of Educational Psychology*, 98(2), p. 438.

Xu, J., 2008. Models of secondary school students' interest in homework: A multilevel analysis. *American Educational Research Journal*, 45(4), pp. 1180-1205.

Xu, J. and Corno, L. 2022. A person-centred approach to understanding self-regulation in homework using latent profile analysis. *Educational Psychology*, 42(6), pp. 767-786.

Zimmerman, B. J., 2000. Attaining self-regulation: A social cognitive perspective. In: M. Boekaerts, P. R. Pintrich and M. Zeidner, eds. *Handbook of Self-Regulation*. Academic Press, pp. 13-39.

Zimmerman, B. J. and Kitsantas, A. 2005. Homework practices and academic achievement: The mediating role of self-efficacy and perceived responsibility beliefs. *Contemporary Educational Psychology*, 30(4), pp. 397-417.

# 2 How Do We Learn?

When I first started to teach, I had very little idea about how we learn. As a result, the way I explained concepts (mostly through pre-prepared PowerPoint slides) or the tasks I gave my students (worksheet overload) were sub-optimal at best and detrimental to their learning at worst. This was reflected in the homework I set too, with tasks that were set mainly to follow a policy and with very little thought as to its impact on student learning.

In their book exploring the evidence base for homework, Hallam and Rogers state that homework must be an integral part of the instruction and learning taking place in the classroom for it to have a positive impact on student attainment (Hallam, 2018). Having a strong understanding of how we learn is therefore a vital prerequisite to setting homework that has any benefit on student outcomes.

There is extensive literature, books and articles, that explain our current understanding of how learning takes place in minute detail. What follows is a brief summary of the key principles of how we learn. These will inform how we design, plan and set effective homework (Chapter 3).

## Memory

Our understanding of how memory works has come a long way over the years from believing they were really traces of our past selves in the time of Plato to thinking we were born with a blank slate and our sensory experiences developed our memories (the tabula rasa theory by John Locke).

DOI: 10.4324/9781003434986-3

Today, we know that we have an unlimited long-term memory and a working memory with limited capacity. We temporarily hold information in our working memories whilst we process it. Figure 2.1 shows how the two types of memory work to allow us to process, encode, store and retrieve information.

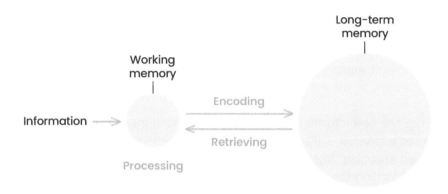

*Figure 2.1* A simple diagram showing how new information is processed, encoded and retrieved.

New information enters the working memory, where it is processed. Our working memory has a severely limited capacity so it is important that only the information we want our students to process enters their working memories.

## What You Attend to Is What You Learn

This statement (Mccrea, 2019), together with the now famous 'memory is the residue of thought' (Willingham, 2008), has changed the way I think about learning completely. In the image above, information that enters our working memory will be processed in some way.

Classrooms tend to be information-rich with events that are both relevant (such as all the content we are teaching them) and irrelevant (such as the noise of a music lesson from next door) competing for space in our students' working memories. In addition, students may be thinking of events from outside the classroom such as what they might get for lunch from the canteen or how excited they are for the weekend.

Knowing this is incredibly useful to teachers as we understand the limitations of the working memory and how important it is to direct attention to key information within the classroom.

But, this is equally useful to understand in terms of setting effective homework, as we will see in Chapter 3.

Once the new information entering our working memory is processed, in some cases, it is transferred into our long-term memory in a process called encoding. Not all new information is transferred. For example, I was watching the news earlier today, and whilst the information from the news items entered my working memory, only the ones that seemed significant to me will have entered my long-term memory (in this case, it was England winning the fifth Ashes Test match).

One of the reasons I attended to this particular piece of news and, therefore, likely processed it successfully, is because I attributed value to this information (Mccrea, 2019), although it still doesn't mean I enjoy cricket!

If the new information is meaningfully processed, then the encoded material develops long-term connections with our other related memories. This new information is now stored.

Kirschner, Sweller and Clark have beautifully and succinctly defined learning as being a change in long-term memory. They say that 'if nothing has changed in long-term memory, nothing has been learned' (Kirschner, 2006).

Another useful definition of learning by Coe is 'Learning happens when people have to think hard' (Coe, 2013).

Even if the information is encoded into long-term memory, it may still be inaccessible because forgetting happens all the time.

The work of a German psychologist, Hermann Ebbinghaus, on memory is considered groundbreaking. In 1880, Ebbinghaus conducted experiments on himself to understand memory better. He focused on memorising and recall of nonsensical words such as 'TUV' and 'YAT' to avoid any existing associations that might influence memory. His work led to the development of what we now call Ebbinghaus' forgetting curve, which shows the decline of retention of learnt material over time (Figure 2.2).

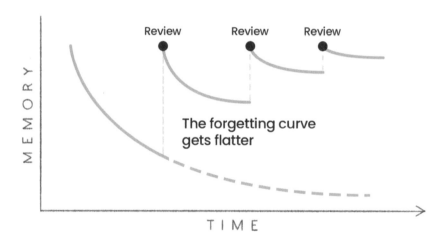

*Figure 2.2*  A depiction of Ebbinghaus' forgetting curve by InnerDrive.

## *A Note of Caution Over the Forgetting Curve*

Although Ebbinghaus' work has been successfully replicated (Murre, 2015), it has been criticised over the years due to its artificial nature, lack of real-world relevance and lack of meaning associated with the learnt information – when we learn something new, we can usually tether it to *existing* knowledge.

## Organising Knowledge

Every time we come across new information, we create or modify a 'schema' within our memories. Schema Theory was first proposed by a British psychologist, Sir Frederic Bartlett, in the 1930s, and described in his seminal work 'Remembering: A Study in Experimental and Social Psychology'.

Figure 2.3 shows schemata in our memories and how a new piece of information may be attached to an existing schema.

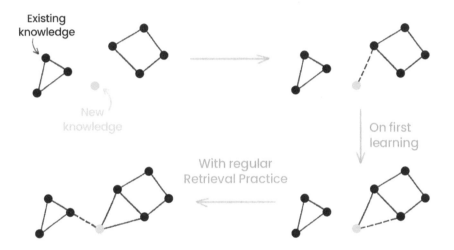

*Figure 2.3* Diagram showing how new knowledge forms connections with existing knowledge and how these connections are strengthened through regular retrieval practice.

## The Importance of Prior Knowledge or What You Already Know Influences New Learning

Learning happens when the student can relate new information to an existing schema and is most successful when done in a meaningful way. David Ausubel, an American psychologist, stated that teachers should focus on facilitating meaningful learning by helping students relate new information to their existing schemata through the use of Advance Organisers. These provide a structured way of relating new and existing bodies of knowledge.

Interestingly, Ausubel's theory of assimilation provides a distinction between more or less meaningful forgetting. If students have developed well-structured and meaningful cognitive structures during initial learning, they are more likely to experience meaningful forgetting, which leaves a trace of the memory and therefore makes it easier for the student to re-learn the information again (Cottingham, 2023).

## Generative Learning

First proposed in the 1970s and expanded on by Fiorella and Mayer, generative learning is important for learners to make sense of new information. They do this by selecting the information to focus on, mentally organising it and integrating it with the relevant prior knowledge. This is known as the Selecting-Organising-Integrating (SOI) model of learning (Fiorella, 2016). This chimes with what we know about cognitive science: what we attend to is what we learn (*selecting*), and we build schemata and make meaning by *organising* and *integrating* new information with existing knowledge.

Fiorella and Mayer studied the literature and identified eight strategies that promote generative learning and therefore meaning-making: summarising, mapping, drawing, imagining, self-testing, self-explaining, teaching and enacting, with some working best for novices, whilst others are better for expert learners (Fiorella, 2015).

## Novices Versus Experts

Learners can be broadly classified into two categories: novice and experts. Contrary to past belief, a novice is not a little expert but someone who has limited or poorly organised schemata in a specific domain (Kirschner, 2020).

I am a biology specialist and so consider myself an expert in biology teaching. If I was asked to teach history, whilst I would be familiar with a portion of the content due to some overlap with biology, I would definitely be a novice.

Due to the way knowledge is organised in our memories, novices tend to encode information superficially and have less structured cognitive structures. In contrast, experts have rich connections within their schemata in a domain and can encode information at a deeper level (Ifenthaler, 2011).

Another consideration here is that when novices process new information, their already severely limited working memory could get overloaded. At some stage, though, with plenty of practise and retrieval, schemata can be automatically processed. This is when a novice becomes an expert.

The expertise reversal effect, therefore, comes into play when teaching. For a novice, explicit guidance and instruction are required to help mitigate the limited capacity of their working memory and to help them process new information.

However, if this type of guidance and instruction is given to expert learners, there is a danger that some or all of the guidance is redundant. This could place an unnecessary load on their working memory (Kalyuga, 2003).

## Problem-Solving for Conceptual Knowledge?

Several studies that provide evidence for the beneficial effect of explicit instruction on learning tend to focus on procedural knowledge (such as in mathematics) (Chen, 2021). On the other hand, when it comes to conceptual knowledge, problem-solving followed by explicit instruction (Problem-Solving-Instruction or PS-I) seems to be more effective in terms of learning measures such as transfer (Loibl, 2016). This PS-I approach is what the concept of productive failure proposes: learners attempt solving a problem they have not been taught, followed by explicit instruction on their solutions and strategies (Kapur, 2008).

Successful design of the PS-I approach involves careful consideration of prior knowledge. If the task is completely new to the learner, then there are no benefits to this approach (Loibl, 2016). It has been theorised that the reason PS-I works well with conceptual knowledge is that learners activate relevant prior knowledge during the problem-solving phase. Even if they do not find a viable solution to the problem, the act of retrieving relevant knowledge supports the explicit instruction phase that follows.

Yet another factor is element interactivity. Learning is affected by the number of elements a learner needs to process in their working memory at any one time. This is referred to as element interactivity and it depends on the level of expertise of the learner and the complexity of the task at hand. Ashman et al. found that for higher element interactivity, explicit instruction first (Instruction-Problem-Solving or I-PS) was superior for both similar and transfer procedural knowledge questions (Ashman, 2020). In contrast, Chen et al. determined that there was no significant difference between I-PS and PS-I sequences for conceptual knowledge of either low- or high-element interactivity (Chen, 2021).

When it comes to learning, it is apparent that consideration must be given to the type of knowledge (procedural versus conceptual) as well as the element interactivity (level of expertise of the learner and complexity of the task). In general, if the task is complex, requires a lot of processing or prior knowledge is insufficient, explicit instruction first is important for learning. If, on the other hand, the task is based on conceptual knowledge, is straightforward, doesn't require much processing or prior knowledge is high, then a problem-solving first approach may benefit learning.

## Making Things Difficult but Not Too Difficult

Forgetting does not mean the memory is lost. Memories can be retrieved with the right, high-quality cues (Willingham, 2008). Practising retrieval often helps us create stronger connections between concepts and build and consolidate effective pathways (Furst, 2022).

Bjork and Bjork describe our memory as having two strengths: storage strength and retrieval strength (Bjork, 2020). The diagram below is my attempt to explain the difference between these two types of strengths.

Novices, therefore, would likely have lower storage and retrieval strengths for knowledge in a domain compared to experts.

So, as teachers, our aim is to increase both the storage and retrieval strength of key knowledge.

But in order to increase storage strength, retrieval strength needs to be low. If retrieval strength is high, then we don't need to put in much effort to retrieve anything. This has a minimal impact on storage strength and therefore not much learning is taking place.

Effective homework can play an important role in increasing storage strength by making retrieval difficult but not too difficult.

Fortunately for us, Robert Bjork coined a convenient and alliterative phrase: 'desirable difficulties'. To clarify the meaning of the word 'desirable', Bjork and Bjork have stated:

> Desirable difficulties, versus the array of undesirable difficulties, are desirable because they trigger encoding and retrieval processes that support learning, comprehension, and remembering. If, however, the learner does not have the background knowledge or skills to respond to them successfully, they become undesirable difficulties.
>
> (Bjork, 2011)

The right level of challenge is necessary to provide these desirable difficulties. How do we work out how to provide this right type of challenge?

Frederick Reif, a physicist and psychologist, wrote a book called *Applying Cognitive Science to Education*, which provided an incredible guide to using the principles of cognitive science to teach effectively. In his book, he introduced an equation (he *was* a physicist, after all) to determine the level of challenge of a task.

Adam Boxer (2021) (also a lover of equations) has modified it to include components that can either increase or decrease cognitive load:

$$Challenge \propto \frac{task\ quantity + abstraction}{prior\ knowledge + external\ supports}$$

Task quantity: how many things does the student need to do to complete the task? (high = high challenge)

Abstraction: the more abstract the content, the harder it is to understand

Prior knowledge: how much relevant information does the student recall? (low = high challenge)

External supports: what resources has the student got access to? (low = high challenge)

When we set effective homework, we need to consider these components to ensure it has the right level of challenge. In Chapter 3, we will look at examples (and non-examples) of homework tasks that pose the right level of challenge.

## Retrieval Practice

The goal of teaching is long-term retention and understanding of the material we teach. In order for understanding to occur, students need to first retain key information and build schemata with strong connections between them. This is the prior knowledge in the challenge equation above – students need to have a high prior knowledge in order to call on it when applying it to new contexts.

The act of mapping, summarising, comparing or other generative learning strategies that encourage long-term retention all rely on robust bodies of prior knowledge. Retrieval practice is the key to building and consolidating this prior knowledge.

This may seem contradictory to students revising for an assessment where they feel there are benefits to re-reading or cramming. The thing is there *are* benefits to these strategies but these are short-lived. In school, I remember cramming just before I walked into the hall to do my exam. On more than one occasion, it has helped me retain information needed immediately in the exam. But short-term performance through strategies such as cramming does not equate long-term learning even if it *feels* like it does (Kornell, 2009).

Forgetting is actually really important in consolidating and developing our long-term memory. When we forget something and then make the effort to retrieve it in the future, it is better embedded into our long-term memory (Bjork, 2020).

There is a wealth of evidence supporting the use of retrieval practice in consistently and effectively enhancing learning (Agarwal, 2021).

Crucially, *regular* retrieval practice through testing is far more effective at developing long-term retention than retrieval practice done just the once or re-studying something (Roediger, 2006, 2011). This testing does not mean formal assessments. They can mean quizzes that allow students to practise retrieval of key information.

## Spacing and Interleaving

Besides occurring regularly, there is another strategy that can make retrieval practice effective at long-term knowledge retention – spacing it out. This is also known as distributed practice and is one of the most effective learning strategies a student could employ (Dunlosky, 2013).

Spaced retrieval practice is effortful and makes us feel like we are not learning but, in actual fact, not only does it improve long-term retention but also increases *transfer* or application of knowledge to new contexts (Carpenter, 2019).

Interleaving, where concepts are practised in a mixed order instead of sequentially, has also been shown to have promise in long-term retention of knowledge (Dunlosky, 2013). Busch et al. remind us that when employing interleaving, the most benefit is obtained when the concepts are from the same subject and are subtly related to each other. In this way, students have to think hard about which strategies to employ to answer the question instead of simply applying the same principles to questions that require the same strategies (Busch, 2023). Figure 2.4 depicts the ways in which interleaving can be made more effective in learning.

**Blocking** involves doing Concept 1, then Concept 2, then Concept 3.

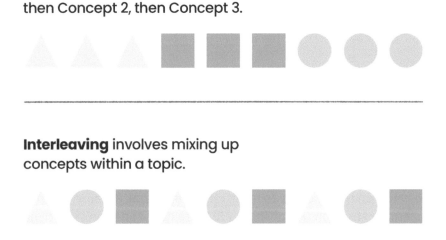

**Interleaving** involves mixing up concepts within a topic.

*Figure 2.4* Diagram showing interleaving involving mixing up concepts within a topic compared to blocking information.

## Feedback

Corrective feedback has been proven to enhance the effect of retrieval practice (or the testing effect) on long-term retention but there is still some benefit when feedback is not provided (Roediger, 2011).

But when retrieval practice success is low, repeated feedback can *reverse* the testing effect. To circumvent this, regular retrieval practice can improve retrieval success, which, in turn, means that feedback is beneficial rather than detrimental (Racsmány, 2020).

The combined effect of successful retrieval practice and corrective feedback is purported to be due to students feeling motivated to learn (Abel, 2020).

In fact, a recent study found that neutral or positive feedback significantly increased self-efficacy, which, in turn, increased the benefits of retrieval practice, compared to negative feedback (Frankenstein, 2022).

Providing feedback can show students that teachers value their effort and that there is a possibility to improve – an incorrect answer is not final, it can be altered for the future.

Taken together, this has important implications for retrieval practice and the feedback we provide our students, both within the classroom and through homework.

## Cognitive Science Principles for Learning

There is quite a bit of research into how we learn, as a result of which we better understand how to teach effectively. Barak Rosenshine's principles of instruction (Rosenshine, 2012) are based on cognitive science theories and findings. These principles are replicated as follows:

1) Begin a lesson with a short review of previous learning.
2) Present new material in small steps with student practice.
3) Ask a large number of questions and check the responses of all students.
4) Provide models.
5) Guide student practice.
6) Check for student understanding.
7) Obtain a high success rate.
8) Provide scaffolding for difficult tasks.

9)  Require and monitor independent practice.

10)  Engage students in weekly and monthly reviews.

At least half of these principles can be applied to homework. Independent practice and frequent reviews of learning are key principles because they help students learn and retain knowledge better.

If you have never really read about any of the principles discussed in this chapter, you will most certainly feel that your own working memory is overloaded. To help with this, below are the six main principles in the form of statements to consider when we want to set effective homework. These statements will form the basis of Chapter 3.

•   Retrieval of knowledge needs to have low retrieval strength (increase forgetting) in order to increase storage strength (increase long-term retention).

•   Retrieval practice needs to happen regularly.

•   Retrieval practice needs to be spaced apart or distributed over time.

•   Challenge must be at the right level depending on whether the student is a novice or an expert. This needs to take into consideration the type of knowledge and the element interactivity.

•   Feedback enhances the benefits of retrieval practice.

## Chapter Summary

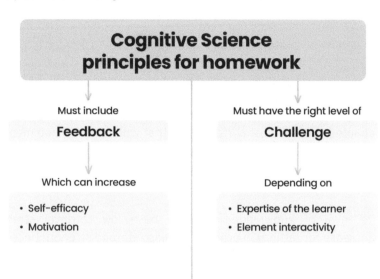

**Cognitive Science principles for homework**

Must include
### Feedback

Which can increase
- Self-efficacy
- Motivation

Must have the right level of
### Challenge

Depending on
- Expertise of the learner
- Element interactivity

Must incorporate
### Retrieval Practice

Which is most effective when
- Regular
- Allows for forgetting to take place
- Spaced and distributed over time

# References

Abel, M. and Bäuml, K-H. T. 2020. Would you like to learn more? Retrieval practice plus feedback can increase motivation to keep on studying. *Cognition*, 201, pp. 1-8.

Agarwal, P. K., Nunes, L. D. and Blunt, J. R., 2021. Retrieval practice consistently benefits student learning: A systematic review of applied research in schools and classrooms. *Educational Psychology Review*, 33, pp. 1409-1453.

Ashman, G., Kalyuga, S. and Sweller, J., 2020. Problem-solving or explicit instruction: Which should go first when element interactivity is high? *Educational Psychology Review*, 32, pp. 229-247.

Bjork, E. and Bjork R., 2011. Making things hard on yourself, but in a good way: Creating desirable difficulties to enhance learning. In: M. A. Gernsbacher, R. W. Pew, L. M. Hough and J. R. Pomerantz, eds. *Psychology and the Real World: Essays Illustrating Fundamental Contributions to Society*. Worth Publishers, pp. 56-64.

Bjork, R. A. and Bjork, E. L., 2020. Desirable difficulties in theory and practice. *Journal of Applied Research in Memory and Cognition*, 9(4), pp. 475-479.

Boxer, A., 2021. *Teaching Secondary Science: A Complete Guide*. John Catt Educational Ltd.

Busch, B., Watson, E. and Bogatchek, L., 2023. *Teaching & Learning Illuminated: The Big Ideas, Illustrated*. Routledge.

Carpenter, S. K. and Agarwal, P. K., 2019. *How to use spaced retrieval practice to boost learning*. (Online) Available at: retrievalpractice.org (Accessed 3 August 2023).

Chen, O., Woolcott, G. and Kalyuga, S., 2021. Comparing alternative sequences of examples and problem-solving tasks: the case of conceptual knowledge. *The Educational and Developmental Psychologist*, 38(1), pp. 158-170.

Coe, R., 2013. *Improving Education: A Triumph of Hope Over Experience*. Inaugural Lecture of Professor Robert Coe, Durham University.

Cottingham, S., 2023. *Ausubel's Meaningful Learning in Action*. John Catt Educational Ltd.

Dunlosky, J., 2013. Strengthening the Student Toolbox: Study Strategies to boost learning. *American Educator*, 37(3), pp. 12-21.

Fiorella, L. and Mayer, R. E., 2015. *Learning as a Generative Activity: Eight Learning Strategies that Promote Understanding.* Cabridge University Press.

Fiorella, L. and Mayer, R. E., 2016. Eight ways to promote generative learning. *Educational Psychology Review*, 28, pp. 717–741.

Frankenstein, A. Udeogu, O. J., McCurdy, M. P., Sklenar, A. and Leshikar, E., 2022. Exploring the relationship between retrieval practice, self-efficacy, and memory. *Memory and Cognition*, 50, pp. 1299–1318.

Furst, E., 2022. *Learning in the brain.* (Online) Available at: https://sites.google.com/view/efratfurst/learning-in-the-brain?pli=1 (Accessed 31 July 2023).

Hallam, S. and Rogers, L., 2018. *Homework: The Evidence.* 2nd ed. London: UCL Institute of Education Press.

Ifenthaler, D., Masduki, I. and Seel, N. M.2011. The mystery of cognitive structure and how we can detect it: tracking the development of cognitive structures over time. *Instructional Science*, 39, pp. 41–61.

Kalyuga, S., Ayres, P., Chandler, P. and Sweller, J., 2003. The expertise reversal effect. *Educational Psychologist*, 38(1), pp. 23–31.

Kapur, M., 2008. Productive failure. *Cognition and Instruction*, 26(3), pp. 379–424.

Kirschner, P. A. and Hendrick, C., 2020. A novice is not a little expert. In: *How Learning Happens.* Oxford: Routledge, pp. 4–12.

Kirschner, P. A., Sweller, J. and Clark, R. E., 2006. Why minimal guidance during instruction does not work: An analysis of the failure of constructivist, discovery, problem-based, experiential, and inquiry-based teaching. *Educational Psychologist*, 41(2), pp. 75–86.

Kornell, N., 2009. Optimising learning using flashcards: Spacing is more effective than cramming. *Applied Cognitive Psychology*, 23, pp. 1297–1317.

Loibl, K., Roll, I. and Rummel, N., 2016. Towards a theory of when and how problem solving followed by instruction supports learning. *Educational Psychology Review*, 29, pp. 693–715.

Mccrea, P., 2019. Learning: What it is, and how might we catalyse it? Ambition Institute. (Online) Available at: https://s3.eu-west-2.amazonaws.com/ambition-institute/documents/Learning_what_is_it_and_how_might_we_catalyse_it_v1.4.pdf (Accessed July 2023).

Murre, J. M. J. and Dros, J., 2015. Replication and analysis of Ebbinghaus' forgetting curve. *PLOS One*, 10(7), p. e0120644.

Racsmány, M., Szőllősi, Á. and Marián, M., 2020. Reversing the testing effect by feedback is a matter of performance criterion at practice. *Memory and Cognition*, 48(7), pp. 1161–1170.

Roediger, H. L. and Butler, A. C., 2011. The critical role of retrieval practice in long-term retention. *Trends in Cognitive Sciences*, 15(1), pp. 20–27.

Roediger, H. L. and Karpicke, J. D., 2006. Test-enhanced learning: Taking memory tests improves long-term retention. *Psychological Science*, 17(3), pp. 249–255.

Rosenshine, B., 2012. Principles of instruction: Research-based strategies that all teachers should know. *American Educator*, 36(1), p. 12.

Willingham, D. T., 2008. What will improve a student's memory? *American Educator*, 32(4), pp. 17–25.

# 3 Making Homework Effective

So far, we have seen:

- In Chapter 1, that the evidence base for homework is unclear due to the variability in homework tasks and the disproportionate number of studies focused solely on mathematics homework. Despite this, there is *some* evidence of better outcomes when homework is done by students.

- In Chapter 2, that there is a wealth of evidence about how we learn, and understanding this helps us teach, and students learn more effectively.

Based on the evidence in Chapter 2, we have the following six principles of evidence-based strategies to increase long-term retention:

- Retrieval practice needs to happen regularly.

- Retrieval of knowledge needs to have low retrieval strength (increase forgetting) in order to increase storage strength (increase long-term retention).

- Retrieval practice needs to be spaced apart or distributed over time.

- Challenge must be at the right level depending on whether the student is a novice or an expert. This needs to take into consideration the type of knowledge and the element interactivity.

- Feedback enhances the benefits of retrieval practice.

DOI: 10.4324/9781003434986-4

These principles need to be implemented in the classroom to encourage long-term retention of knowledge and, eventually, a deep understanding of our subjects.

All the research on effective homework suggests that it must be an integral part of the learning in the classroom (Cooper, 1989; Hallam, 2018; Bempechat, 2019; EEF, 2021). Therefore, it follows that the same principles of learning we listed above need to be applied to homework to achieve the same outcomes.

## Types of Homework

Studies tend to group homework tasks into three main categories: practice, preparation and extension (Doyle, 1990), but there are other forms of tasks that tend to be set. Table 3.1 summarises these different tasks, what the evidence says about their use as homework and which group of learners will most benefit from the type of homework.

## What About Computer-Based Homework Tasks?

A number of teachers now set homework through a computer-based platform such as MyMaths, Carousel Learning or Google Forms quizzes. The benefits of using such platforms include immediate support (in the form of videos or web pages) and immediate feedback on student responses.

A systematic review of research into the use of online homework compared to traditional homework for mathematics, sciences and business found that over half of the studies showed neutral effects on achievement. This is despite the fact that students in these studies preferred the online homework over traditional homework. Additionally, it was suggested that whilst online homework may have the same effect as traditional homework on achievement, it could potentially save teachers a lot of time with setting and providing feedback (Magalhães, 2020).

*Table 3.1* Exploration of what the evidence says about different types of homework tasks.

| Type of homework | What is it? | What does the evidence say? | Who would benefit from this type of homework? |
|---|---|---|---|
| **Retrieval practice** | Tasks that involve recalling information from memory. | Retrieval practice has been shown to consolidate learning and encourage long-term retention of information (Agarwal, 2021). | **Novices and experts.** With novices, the retrieval practice must be focused on key knowledge, whilst for experts, it should be focused on elaboration and application. |
| **Preparation (e.g. pre-reading, flipped learning)** | Tasks that involve pre-reading or watching material that will be later covered in the classroom. | Synthesis of the research by Hallam and Rogers suggests that preparation-type homework tasks are the most effective in terms of student achievement. Flipped learning seems to be effective at motivating students and increasing attainment but is best when students definitely undertake the preparatory work, a lot of care is taken to ensure tasks are not too difficult and there are several chances for small group feedback sessions (Hallam, 2018). | **Experts.** Novices lack sophisticated schemata (Kalyuga, 2003). They learn little when exposed to new information (Didau, 2018) and could make incorrect meaning if understanding is not checked and addressed immediately (Cottingham, 2023). Experts, on the other hand, will have well-structured and connected schemata. They can gain a lot from independent work such as pre-reading for which they have already achieved mastery (Didau, 2018). |

*(continued)*

*Table 3.1* (continued)

| Type of homework | What is it? | What does the evidence say? | Who would benefit from this type of homework? |
|---|---|---|---|
| **Extension** | Tasks that involve applying or transferring learning to new contexts. Also known as application or problem-solving tasks. | Extension tasks that involve applying key skills to a different style of question significantly improved mathematics test scores in lower secondary students (Rosario, 2015). | **Experts.** Without the pre-requisite knowledge required to answer certain types of questions, novices will struggle to transfer relevant knowledge to new situations and contexts. |
| **Generative learning** | Tasks that involve students to select, organise and integrate information (SOI model) (Fiorella, 2016). | Evidence shows that generative learning strategies such as mapping, self-testing and self-explanation support schema building in students, helping them achieve better understanding (Enser, 2020). | **Novices (with lots of practice and guidance) and experts.** Some tasks such as mapping could be beneficial to novices to help relate facts to each other but to be effective at enhancing learning, each of the strategies need to be practised sufficiently in the classroom (Enser, 2020). |

*(continued)*

*Table 3.1* (continued)

| Type of homework | What is it? | What does the evidence say? | Who would benefit from this type of homework? |
|---|---|---|---|
| **Research/ projects** | Tasks that involve finding information and presenting or summarising it. | Projects and research tasks can increase motivation and provide links to real-life applications of curriculum content (Sadlier, 2011). Having projects that can be referred to in the classroom over weeks has also been shown to motivate students to do more homework and feel involved in their work (Hallam, 2018). | **Experts.** We already know that novices in a domain struggle to integrate new information due to unsophisticated schemata. Researching information when retention of foundational knowledge is not secure could result in, at best, surface-level work and, at worst, completely irrelevant work. For example, a student researching 'in vitro fertilisation' online might find the following and copy it: 'Assisted reproduction is currently used by nearly one in every five couples in the Czech Republic. Infertility issues are on the rise and the number of children born through IVF has grown rapidly in the last decade. IVF consists of many treatment methods, from fairly simple procedures to more complex treatments with laboratory assistance'. Not all students would copy without thought but there is a high possibility of this happening if the student a) doesn't understand the topic well and b) doesn't value the homework. |

In a different analysis of the research, Hallam and Rogers found that computer-based homework tasks where feedback was provided had a greater impact on achievement, particularly in lower-performing students (Hallam, 2018).

## Does Student Choice Enhance the Effectiveness of Homework?

Homework efficacy does not just relate to the type of task. Other factors can have a significant impact on how effective a homework task is. For instance, if students don't have sufficient resources (either mental or physical) to draw upon, then the complexity of the homework is too high and the homework is unlikely to have benefits on student outcomes.

One factor that has been proposed time and again is student choice. When people have choice and control over their actions, they tend to feel they have autonomy, which is a key driver of motivation (Ryan, 2000).

Patall et al. reported that when students were allowed to choose between two similar homework tasks, they were more intrinsically motivated, completed more homework and did better on their assessment compared to students who were not given a choice of tasks. It was, however, noted that for teachers, this added significantly to their workload (Patall, 2010).

So, the choice of homework tasks would serve to motivate our students so that they do more homework and achieve better. But we know that students are not the best at choosing the right strategies that help them learn best (Dunlosky, 2013).

A meta-analysis of choice and intrinsic motivation revealed that *irrelevant* choice had the strongest effect on motivating students. This means that providing choices on things that are unrelated to the instruction or learning can motivate students.

Another aspect of choice is something called *perceived* choice. This is where students feel like they have a choice and, therefore, autonomy.

If we offer two homework tasks: one which involves effort and thinking and another that is perceived as simpler, most students will inevitably choose the latter.

Helping students see the value in the homework being set and explicitly explaining why the task will help will provide students with a more autonomous feeling than if we set work that appears challenging but is perceived as controlling by the teacher.

Additionally, as students progress in their level of expertise from complete novice to more of an expert in a domain, including an element of choice in homework may promote intrinsic motivation.

## Principles of Effective Homework

What makes effective homework? We can derive some principles based on the following three things:

- Evidence on homework and its impact on student outcomes.

- Principles of long-term retention and understanding.

- Efficacy of homework tasks depending on the level of expertise of the student.

Here are the six principles of effective homework:

- Homework should be set regularly. More homework equates to better outcomes but too much is counterproductive.

- Homework should initially and primarily incorporate retrieval practice with changes to the type of homework as students progress in their expertise in a certain domain.

- Novice learners should mostly have tasks that focus on increasing the retrieval strength of key knowledge and schema building. Expert learners should mostly have tasks that focus on applying key knowledge to new contexts.

- Questions/tasks on content should be spaced over time to allow forgetting to happen.

- Feedback should be provided to enhance the effectiveness of homework.

- Information from completed homework should inform future teaching and homework tasks.

## Model for Effective Homework

In 1999, Cowan and Hallam proposed a model of homework, outlining all the factors that modulate its impact on student outcomes (Hallam, 2006).

I have adapted and simplified parts of their model to include key factors that must be considered to make homework effective.

The key outcome of effective homework is student access. There is an element of success in determining if students can access the work. Homework must be desirably difficult: students must be able to achieve some success but need to truly think about the work and feel challenged.

This is obviously not an easy feat. A model for homework is useful in designing and implementing effective homework.

Firstly, we can divide homework completion into three sections:

### *Pre-homework*

Before anything else, the purpose of the homework task must be determined. Without purpose, there is no direction. None of the other factors needed for effective homework will be valid if there is no clear purpose to the task that is set.

In my experience, I have previously set homework for the following reasons:

- To follow the school homework policy.
- To appease parents.

- To keep students busy.

- To complete work done in lessons.

- To help students revise (mainly for an upcoming assessment).

- To help students build habits.

- To practise retrieval.

In March 2023, I asked Teacher Tapp to survey secondary school teachers to find out what their top three reasons for setting homework were. Nearly 6000 teachers responded to say that the top two reasons for setting homework were to practise retrieval and to help students revise. For their third option, teachers chose either 'to help students build habits' or 'to follow the school's homework policy'.

For the first three of the above-mentioned reasons, it is clear how they will benefit the student as a learner.

Retrieval practice is proven to help students remember knowledge in the long term.

Revision will help students achieve better in assessments.

Habit-building will be useful in the present and the future when revising and preparing for major assessments or projects.

It is difficult to justify setting homework to follow a homework policy as being directly beneficial to the student, and, therefore, I suggest this should *not* be the purpose of homework. As we will see in Chapter 4 on motivation, it is important for students to buy-in to the purpose of homework for it to be effective.

The key question to pose to yourself when determining the purpose of homework is: How will this task benefit my students so they improve their long-term retention and understanding?

The *design of the task* is another consideration linked to purpose. Tasks should be designed with the level of expertise of the student in mind ensuring they align with the intended purpose of the assigned home-work. Table 3.1 (see page 40) can help with deciding what type of task is best for different students.

This does not mean we set different tasks for different students pre-cisely pitched at their level of expertise. This is an impossible and counterproductive feat. Impossible because when you have a class of 30 students, it is certainly not sustainable to set 30 different pieces of homework. This then makes it counterproductive as the teacher will be unable to provide the same level of feedback on the home-work each time and the overall efficacy of the homework decreases dramatically.

Realistically, most (if not all) students in our classrooms are novices in a domain. They may become less of a novice as the topic progresses, but as we start working on new content, that level of expertise reverts to the lower end of the novice-expert scale (Figure 3.1).

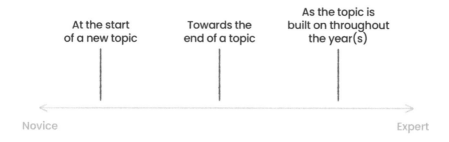

*Figure 3.1* Scale depicting novices moving towards expertise in a domain.

But the purpose and design of the homework are not enough. Students who are given the best possible homework task with a very clear pur-pose may still not gain any benefits from it due to other factors.

One such factor is the *environment* in which the student works. The environment needs to be conducive to learning. Research tells us that this includes a quiet, comfortable space to work in, the right tempera-ture, sufficient lighting and ventilation (Duke, 1998).

Our student has now been set a high-quality piece of work that matches their level of expertise well. They have the right environment to work in. They start working on the task but need to call on their memory or find support for some questions. Where do they look? Have they got reliable resources to depend on?

Imagine a student who has missed a week of school due to illness. They are set homework and feel lost because part of the resources they need are the notes made in the lessons they missed.

Imagine a student who struggles to remember key concepts despite working hard. Where can they look to help them succeed at their homework?

This links to the final factor to consider during the pre-homework stage: access. Can the student physically access the homework? If the homework is an online piece of work, does the student have access to the Internet and a reliable device? If the homework is on a worksheet, what happens if they misplace it or if they miss the lesson where it was handed out?

As discussed earlier, access is not only physical but also mental. Do students know *how* to complete the work? Do they understand the task?

The best way to ensure mental access is by:

- Explicit modelling and practice of similar tasks in the classroom
- Standardising the format of the task

Standardising and practice of a certain format and style of a task makes it more recognisable to students, which means they are more likely to attempt the task (Lemov et al., 2023).

This is not to say that every piece of homework always looks the same. Each time a new format is set, however, it needs to follow sufficient modelling and practice in the classroom. The key here is to ensure students recognise the type of task and know what to do to complete the work.

## During Homework

Our student is now seated at a table, in a quiet, pleasant environment, ready to work. The next factor that affects the efficacy of homework is *time*. More time spent on homework does not always equate to better outcomes (Maltese, 2012). Students working on their General Certificate of Secondary Education (GCSE) in the UK typically study nine subjects. If each subject sets homework that takes an hour to complete each week, this would mean students are expected to spend about an hour and a half on homework per day, including weekends. This is reasonable for most students, but it does not factor in additional revision for assessments, deadlines for coursework, or other academic or non-academic commitments.

If subjects set a lot more homework and/or expect submission in less than a week, then this slowly inches towards being counterproductive. Homework is only effective if students can actually spend time on it whilst not feeling overwhelmed.

Having a clear sense of how much time homework is meant to take and communicating this with students will provide them with sufficient information to organise their time. Additionally, we need to consider homework set by other subjects in order to ensure the tasks we set are effective in terms of time. Finally, it is important to note that some students may take longer on a piece of homework than others.

Intricately linked to time spent on homework is knowing the proportion of that time spent by the student on *thinking* about the task. Is the student focused on the content of the task? Are they distracted by any peripheral aspects of the task such as irrelevant instructions or information?

We need to consider how students get into focus by thinking about the work they are doing so they don't fall into the habit of 'going through the motions'. Practising similar style questions in lessons breeds familiarity with the task, which means the focus is on the content of the task. But this alone could still mean students do the homework without much thought. Discussing the task and posing similar questions in the classroom would provide useful data to the teacher about how much actual thought has gone into completing the work.

And what if they are stuck when working on the task? For some students, it may be easy to give up and say that, at least, they tried. Others may give a cursory glance at their notes or perhaps turn to a search engine for help. Yet some others might spend hours looking for help on the task.

None of these situations is ideal. None will progress the student. We cannot force students not to use a search engine or copy an answer from a book, but we can model to students what they should do when stuck. We can do this successfully in the classroom and make the habit of addressing challenges so routine that our student knows exactly what to do at home.

Ensuring students know where to look for support and what to do with it ties in with the student's self-regulation. Can they persist at a task when they find it challenging? Can they ignore distractions such as their smartphone or the television?

It is impossible for us to recreate the same conditions in the classroom as they would be in each individual student's home. What we can do, as mentioned already, is to model good study behaviours such as silence when thinking and independent work relentlessly in the classroom. It will reach a point where the student associates the process of learning with those same study habits. We can also discuss those successful behaviours following the submission of homework in the classroom.

## Post-homework

Our student has now completed the homework and submitted it. Without consideration of what happens beyond this point, homework could very quickly lose its value and efficacy.

Imagine you have spent a long time working on a report. You have spent time thinking deeply about it and looked up something when you weren't sure about it. You submit your report to your line manager and then … nothing. Perhaps you get an acknowledgement for completing and submitting the report on time but get nothing else. If this happened to me (and it has!), I would feel like the effort I put into the report was pointless. I would think about not putting in as much effort next time as a result.

Effective homework can only be sustained if teachers provide useful *feedback* on the work our students submit.

Feedback serves two purposes (Figure 3.2):

*Figure 3.2* Graphic showing how feedback affects students and the information gathered by teachers about students.

- In order to provide feedback, the teacher obtains useful information about the work put in by the student.

- The very act of providing feedback increases student motivation because they know their effort and work will be recognised.

Both these purposes depend on feedback that can actually help the student and is sustainable for the teacher. The most powerful feedback is one that effects a change in the student's knowledge, habits or thinking. Timing of feedback is important too. Both immediate and delayed feedback have their place (Shute, 2008), but if feedback is provided several days or weeks after the fact then its impact could be severely diminished.

There is a lot of valuable information to be gauged from a piece of sub-mitted homework. Are there any gaps in the student's knowledge? Have they misunderstood something? Do they hold a misconception? Have they clearly copied their answers from another source? Have they written something that potentially lacks understanding but may be technically correct?

Using this information to inform future teaching in the classroom and further homework that is set is true *responsive* teaching. Whilst we can gather much of this information in the classroom, assessing responses to the above questions from work done independently of our teaching influence is more valuable and indicative of the student's personal hab-its and effort.

Finally, we have to consider *accountability*. How do we recognise the efforts put in by our students? How do we praise or sanction them? Chap-ter 7 explores accountability in more detail. In short, if students do not submit any work or they submit sub-standard work, a sanction shows them you are making them accountable for their actions and giving them ownership of their learning. If students have clearly put in a lot of effort, even if the responses aren't quite right or perfect, praise is important for them to see you appreciate their work and the habits they are building.

## Extraneous Factors

There is a lot of thought that goes into effective homework. Other fac-tors can have a significant influence on the efficacy of homework despite excellent planning, implementation and feedback being in place.

### Student Centric Factors

Emotion and motivation can vary day by day but also within the same day. Homework is most effective when students are comfortable, not stressed and ready to focus. Whilst we cannot control these or even influence them, we can ensure that everything else about the homework is familiar and straightforward.

Student prior knowledge, schemata and level of expertise, which will vary depending on the domain being focused on, can also have an impact on homework completion.

## Home and School Centric Factors

Many students really want to do a good job and improve their learning. They may try their best to follow all our instructions and get the most of their homework. Their circumstances and parents' attitudes towards homework and learning can influence their own thinking and attitude.

School culture is yet another mitigating factor in ensuring homework is effective. In a school where homework is treated as something that is valued by all and enhances and progresses learning, students will have more buy-in to the whole process of doing homework. In a school where homework is set as an afterthought or because the policy demands it, or where there is inconsistency in homework implementation in different classrooms, homework loses some of its impact.

Similarly, teaching with a focus on how students learn and providing feedback that drives change can impact the effectiveness of homework.

So our model for effective homework is complex but necessary for us to see the myriad factors that affect homework (Figure 3.3).

This is why homework could be subpar. There is so much to consider and take into account – some of which we have very little influence over. It can be easy to say, 'why bother, then?'.

Because once homework is effective, once a culture is built of valuing homework and its impact on learning, then something incredible happens. Students start to build important habits. They become more confident in the classroom. They feel they have ownership of their own learning. They are *trusted* to practise on their own, away from your direct guidance. In Chapter 4, I will discuss how homework can help to motivate our students, which is not a sentence I thought I'd ever write (or say) 5 years ago!

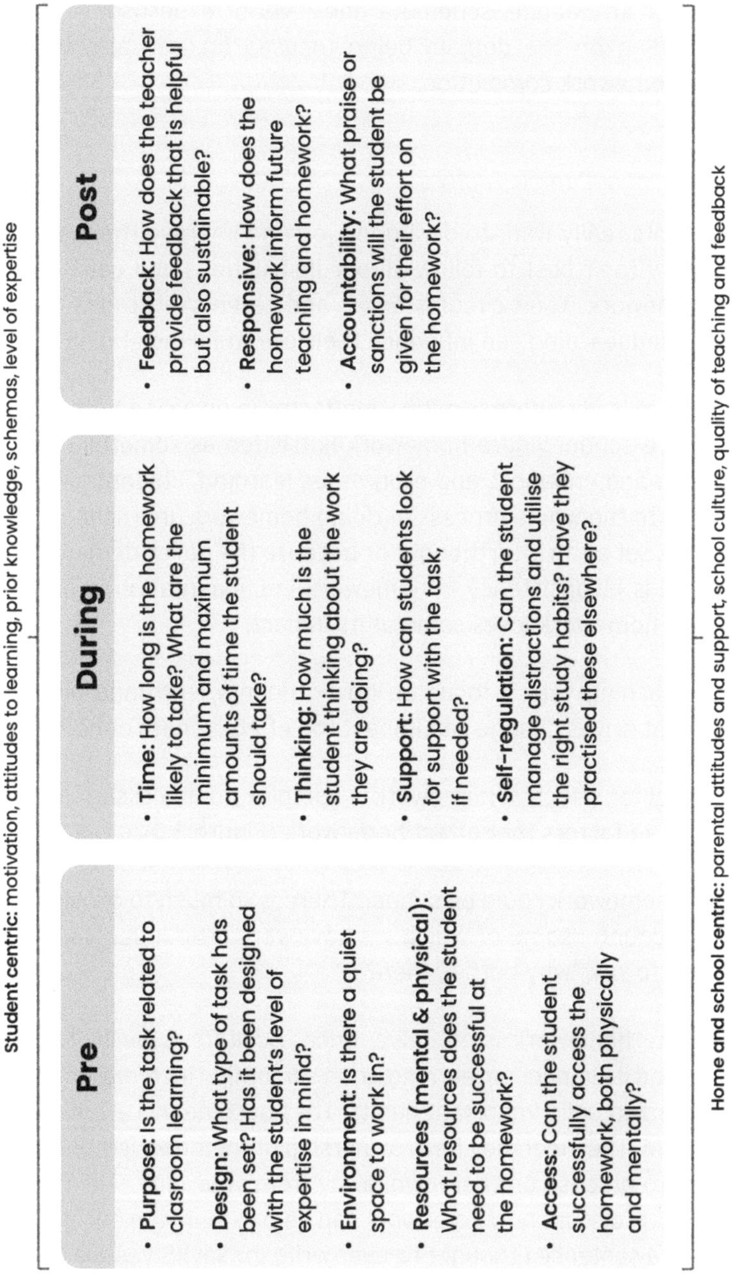

Student centric: motivation, attitudes to learning, prior knowledge, schemas, level of expertise

| Pre | During | Post |
|-----|--------|------|
| • **Purpose:** Is the task related to classroom learning? | • **Time:** How long is the homework likely to take? What are the minimum and maximum amounts of time the student should take? | • **Feedback:** How does the teacher provide feedback that is helpful but also sustainable? |
| • **Design:** What type of task has been set? Has it been designed with the student's level of expertise in mind? | • **Thinking:** How much is the student thinking about the work they are doing? | • **Responsive:** How does the homework inform future teaching and homework? |
| • **Environment:** Is there a quiet space to work in? | • **Support:** How can students look for support with the task, if needed? | • **Accountability:** What praise or sanctions will the student be given for their effort on the homework? |
| • **Resources (mental & physical):** What resources does the student need to be successful at the homework? | • **Self-regulation:** Can the student manage distractions and utilise the right study habits? Have they practised these elsewhere? | |
| • **Access:** Can the student successfully access the homework, both physically and mentally? | | |

Home and school centric: parental attitudes and support, school culture, quality of teaching and feedback

*Figure 3.3* A model for effective homework.

## Chapter Summary

# Effective homework

Must

- Be designed carefully, with the right purpose, support and accountability
- Be set regularly, at the right amount
- Incorporate Retrieval Practice and progress in challenge as student expertise increases
- Space learning over time
- Include feedback so students can improve
- Inform future teaching and homework
- Take student, home and school-related factors into consideration

# References

Agarwal, P. K., Nunes, L. D. and Blunt, J. L., 2021. Retrieval practice consistently benefits student learning: A systematic review of applied research in schools and classrooms. *Educational Psychology Review*, 33, pp. 1409-1453.

Bempechat, J., 2019. The case for (quality) homework: Why it improves learning and how parents can help. *Education Next*, 19(1), pp. 36-43.

Cooper, H., 1989. Synthesis of research on homework. *Educational Leadership*, 47, pp. 85-91.

Cottingham, S., 2023. *Ausubel's Meaningful Learning in Action*. John Catt Educational Ltd.

Didau, D., 2018. *When do novices become experts?* (Online) Available at: https://learningspy.co.uk/psychology/novices-become-experts/ (Accessed August 2023).

Doyle, M. A. E. and Barner B. S., 1990. *Homework as a Learning Experience. What Research Says to the Teacher*. 3rd ed. Washington: National Education Association.

Duke, D. L., 1998. Does it matter where our children learn? *Education*. pp. 2-36. White Paper presented at an Invitational Meeting (Washington, DC, 18 February 1998).

Dunlosky, J., 2013. Strengthening the Student Toolbox: Study strategies to boost learning. *American Educator*, 37(3), pp. 12-21.

EEF, 2021. *Homework*. (Online) Available at: https://educationendowmentfoundation.org.uk/education-evidence/teaching-learning-toolkit/homework#nav-closing-the-disadvantage-gap

Enser, Z. and Enser, M., 2020. *Fiorella and Mayer's Generative Learning in Action*. John Catt Educational Ltd.

Fiorella, L. and Mayer, R. E., 2016. Eight ways to promote generative learning. *Educational Psychology Review*, 28, pp. 717-741.

Hallam, S., 2006. *Homework: Its Uses and Abuses*. London: Institute of Education.

Hallam, S. and Rogers, L., 2018. *Homework: The Evidence*. 2nd ed. London: UCL Institute of Education Press.

Kalyuga, S., Ayres, P., Chandler, P., and Sweller, J., 2003. The expertise reversal effect. *Educational Psychologist*, 38(1), pp. 23-31.

Lemov, D., McCleary, S., Solomon, H. and Woolway, E., 2023. *Teach Like a Champion 3.0: A Practical Resource to Make the 63 Techniques Your Own*. 3rd ed. New Jersey: Jossey-Bass.

Maltese, A. V., Tai, R. H. and Fan, X., 2012. When is homework worth the time? Evaluating the association between homework and achievement in high school science and math. *High School Journal*, 96(1), pp. 52–72.

Magalhães, P., Ferreira, D., Cunha, J. and Rosário P., 2020. Online vs traditional homework: A systematic review on the benefits to students' performance. *Computers and Education*, 152(1).

Patall, E. A., Cooper, H. and Wynn, S. R., 2010. The effectiveness and relative importance of choice in the classroom. *Journal of Educational Psychology*, 102(4), pp. 896–915.

Rosario, P., Núñez,. J. C., Vallejo, G., Cunha, J., Nunes, T., Mourão, R. and Pinto, R., 2015. Does homework design matter? The role of homework's purpose in student mathematics achievement. *Contemporary Educational Psychology*, 43, pp. 10–24.

Ryan, R. M. and Deci, E. L., 2000. Self-determination theory and the facilitation of intrinsic motivation, social development, and well-being. *American Psychologist*, 55(1), p. 68.

Sadlier, H. D., 2011. Homework: What's the point? *International Journal of Learning*, 17(10), pp. 155–163.

Shute, V. J., 2008. Focus on formative feedback. *Review of Educational Research*, 78(1), pp. 153–189.

# 4 Motivating Students Through Homework

Motivation is the Holy Grail of teaching. Imagine a world where *every* student, regardless of interest, felt motivated to do well and extend their learning.

Sadly, this does not tally with the experience of many teachers. Instead, we have some students entering our classrooms with resigned expressions, sighing as they grudgingly pick up their pen to participate in a lesson they have no interest in whatsoever, with whispers of 'I will never need this in my life anyway…'.

Motivation theories are now considered well-established, with school leaders and teachers considering their application in the classroom. Of these theories, two have been researched and revisited numerous times.

Deci and Ryan's self-determination theory (SDT) suggests people need autonomy, competence and relatedness in order to feel motivated (Ryan, 2017). This is applicable to the classroom as motivated students feel that they are in control of their learning and goals (**autonomy**), can actually achieve well (**competence**) and feel a sense of belonging (**relatedness**).

This chimes with the expectancy-value-cost theory of motivation proposed by Barron and Hulleman (Barron, 2015). According to this model, people will feel more motivated if they expect to succeed, can see the

DOI: 10.4324/9781003434986-5

value in doing the task and can allocate time and resources towards it (is it worth the cost?).

Bearing these in mind, consider two students in the same classroom:

Narender listens carefully, follows instructions, does his homework regularly and achieves well in assessments.

Sachin gets distracted easily, tries to follow instructions but usually misses them, forgets to do his homework and doesn't perform as well in assessments.

Narender is more likely to feel motivated because he knows what is required of him to do well, with mastery being an achievable goal, whilst Sachin will feel like he doesn't even belong in that classroom.

But this example is clearly simplistic. Students, and indeed, people in general, can be on various points of the motivation scale (Figure 4.1). In fact, people can feel different levels of motivation on the same day for different tasks or on different days for the same task.

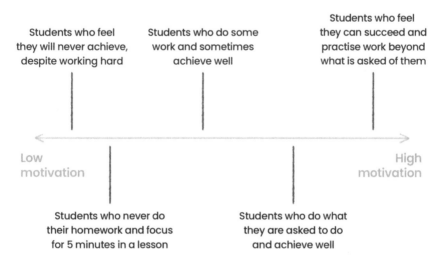

*Figure 4.1* The motivation scale of students in classrooms.

It is no wonder that careful thought is needed to get our students to a place where they can self-motivate each time they work in the classroom. This becomes even more significant when considering out-of-classroom academic activities such as homework. We might be able to influence, encourage and support students within the confines of a well-established classroom. How can we achieve the same when students are in other environments, away from our direct influence?

Consolidating all the research into motivation, Mccrea advises that there are five core drivers to achieve self-motivation status: running consistent routines, securing success, nudging norms, building belonging and boosting buy-in (Mccrea, 2020).

Effective homework and classroom learning need to be cyclical in nature, where each informs and influences the other. In addition to students experiencing success, homework needs to become part of a well-practiced routine with frequent classroom discussions of its value and how it predicts and contributes towards academic success.

Bempechat recommends modelling and practicing self-regulation strategies so these key habits become automated during independent study (Bempechat, 2019).

What could this look like in practice? In order to answer that question, let us consider two classrooms:

| Classroom A | Classroom B |
|---|---|
| Homework is set weekly in the classroom with the purpose of practise, retrieval and application. <br><br> Homework usually takes 15 minutes to complete but as the routine builds, the tasks may take longer. | Homework is only set if the topic demands it. <br><br> If students have fully practised something in the lesson, then homework is not set. |

*(continued)*

| Classroom A | Classroom B |
|---|---|
| The format used for the homework tasks is consistent as well. | The purpose of homework is to consolidate and extend lesson learning. |
| Frequent discussions are held to discuss why a piece of homework is useful and how it links to learning in the classroom, either current or past. | The format of the homework may be similar or different depending on the task set, which depends on the lesson it is linked to. |
| Sanctions are given to students who do not complete the homework, unless there is a legitimate reason. | Discussions about the homework are minimal as the following lesson is based on a different part of the topic. |
| | Sanctions are given to students who do not complete the homework, unless there is a legitimate reason. |

These scenarios are extreme opposites on purpose but in reality classrooms are more likely a mix of the two.

Students in Classroom A can expect a certain style and format of homework and they can expect it to be set regularly. In Classroom B, students don't always know in advance when homework will be set. If they do not complete it, although there are consequences, there may not be time to discuss it properly as the next lesson is taught and a new piece of independent work may be set.

Classroom A follows the five core drivers of motivation (Mccrea, 2020) more closely than Classroom B. There is a higher chance of success as students are continually revisiting past content and skills and forming schemata to link current and past learning. Whilst this may be the case in some instances in Classroom B, this continual revisiting is not routine.

A homework routine becomes well-established and classroom discussions can help nudge the culture towards understanding the value and benefits of homework completion.

## The Importance of Routine

In a survey conducted by Teacher Tapp in March 2023, 16% of around 6000 secondary teachers said they set homework sporadically or less often than once a fortnight.

Let us continue focusing on Narender and Sachin from earlier. Here is a description of each once again:

Narender listens carefully, follows instructions, does his homework regularly and achieves well in assessments.

Sachin gets distracted easily, tries to follow instructions but usually misses them, forgets to do his homework, and doesn't perform as well in assessments.

(A reminder that these are simplistic descriptions and relate to one classroom. Sachin may very well be far more focused in a different subject or outside of school, whilst Narender may struggle elsewhere.)

What would happen if both students received homework sporadically?

| | |
|---|---|
| Narender would most likely not miss an instruction about the homework when it is given.<br><br>Because he is used to doing his homework regularly, he will be used to setting aside time to work independently and may even continue to do so to review the work he has done in lessons. | Sachin struggles to focus in lessons, which means he is more likely to miss an instruction about homework when it is given.<br><br>Because he is not used to doing his homework regularly, he will most likely not make time to review his work unless this is set by the teacher, and even then it may not happen. |

Narender already has the right study habits and if homework is set sporadically, it won't affect him much. With Sachin, on the other hand, if homework is not set regularly, he will fall further behind his peers because he lacks the right habits required to be disciplined with working independently.

What happens if we put both students in a classroom where homework is set regularly?

| | |
|---|---|
| Narender expects homework to be set on a certain day each week/fortnight and probably writes this in his planner in advance of it being set. | Sachin misses some instructions but because the homework is set regularly, he knows that it is always set on the same day each week/fortnight. |
| Even if he misses the lesson when the homework has been set, he knows to expect it and can organise his time. | Even if he misses the lesson when the homework has been set, he knows to expect it. Although he struggles to organise his time, he is more likely to remember and complete the work as the homework is expected each time. |

Now, of course, these scenarios and fictional student descriptions do not represent all situations.

There are students who do listen to instructions but struggle with time. Others listen to instructions but find lessons tricky, and so when they sit down to work, they really need to motivate themselves to complete the work.

For some of these students, setting homework sporadically may mean an occasional reprieve from too much work so they have time and the mental capacity for other activities.

On balance, when considering *all* our students – both the ones that can organise themselves well and those that struggle with this, the benefits of routine homework outweigh those of homework set sporadically. However, teachers need to be mindful of the fact that too much homework routinely can overwhelm and demotivate students (Figure 4.2).

### Sporadic homework

**Pros:**

- Provides students with gaps in work

**Cons:**

- Not expected, so time is difficult to organise.
- Habits require routine, so these are not developed as well.
- May have some instances with lots of homework and others with very little.

### Routine homework

**Pros:**

- Can be expected, even when lessons are missed.
- Time can be organised better.
- Study habits are developed.

**Cons:**

- Could cause students to feel there is no reprieve with work.

*Figure 4.2* The pros and cons of homework set sporadically or routinely.

## Helping Students Feel Successful

Narender and Sachin are both being set homework routinely. But a routine isn't everything. Sachin could know exactly when homework is set and due; he may be able to organise his time well, but he still doesn't feel like he is successful at all in his work. Perhaps, he is working on the homework each time, but his assessment results are not improving at all.

Let us analyse all the steps students need to complete to actually do their homework:

- Organise their time.

- Prepare a place to work quietly.

- Turn off devices or move away from things that may distract.

- Access the homework, e.g. a worksheet that wasn't stuck in or inputting their password correctly.

- Read the instructions carefully.

- Complete all the parts of the homework.

- Think about the homework whilst working on it.

- Submit the homework or stick the sheet in their book.

A lot of the steps that students need to follow are not even directly related to the homework task itself, but they make the completion of homework more likely. Many students may successfully complete homework but may still not gain any benefits from it.

This is because successful homework is not just completed homework. There have been many times in my career where if students submitted homework, then I was delighted. I didn't actually consider if students spent time *thinking* about the homework.

This is the key ingredient: if students spend time thinking about the homework, actively retrieving knowledge and applying it, only then is there an impact on learning and schema building.

If Narender spends an hour on homework, completing it perfectly, following all instructions and presenting it neatly but has not spent much time **actively thinking** about the work, then he is honing skills in the illusion of work but not learning.

From Chapter 3, we know that homework is only effective when it involves learning, otherwise it is just work for the sake of work.

So when it comes to motivation and success, students may feel successful for reasons that may not progress them at all – they are performing but not learning (Soderstrom, 2015).

### How Do We Make Students Feel Successful Whilst Thinking?

My son, N, loves football. He trains three times a week and plays a match at least once a week. He is slight whilst a few of his teammates look older and stronger than him.

Nearly every morning, my husband gets N to train by doing squats, balancing, shuttle runs, etc. It is so hard for N to feel motivated during these morning sessions. Even though we tell him that balancing will help him score better goals, he cannot see the benefits immediately and so he struggles to focus or put in a lot of effort.

This is very similar to asking students to think hard when the benefits of doing so are not immediately obvious to them.

It is a long game. Teachers and students need to be prepared to work at incorporating deep thinking, feeling like this is a challenge and there is little progress in the short term and then see gains in the future.

This brings us back to the challenge equation adapted by Adam Boxer that we explored in Chapter 2.

$$Challenge \propto \frac{task\ quantity + abstraction}{prior\ knowledge + external\ supports}$$

Reducing challenge and cognitive load is not our goal. Our goal is to modulate both so that students are actively thinking about the task.

Active, hard thinking needs extensive practise. This should happen pre-dominantly in the classroom so students know how to persist at something when it gets tough.

The tasks we set should *require* thinking, i.e. they should not be too easy such that students do the task mindlessly.

The best way to figure out the right level of challenge is to gather as much data as possible from your students in the classroom. We can do this by:

- Asking lots of questions where the participation ratio is high. Using mini-whiteboards or other whole-class questioning techniques to provide useful data about what students know and understand.

- Varying the type of questions asked. If we ask a question about a piece of knowledge in exactly the same way each time, the data we gather are not as useful as if we vary the ways in which we assess recall and understanding of the same piece of knowledge.

- Looking at responses to homework and other independent work. How students respond to independent work with *and* without your direct influence is valuable data to inform your teaching and design of future questions.

Homework can be fully integrated into learning done in the classroom by ensuring the focus is on *thinking*, probing this thinking in the classroom and then setting tasks at the right level of challenge.

## 'Doing Homework Is the Norm'

We've got our students into a great routine of doing their homework. Some are even deeply and actively thinking about it. How does this now become the norm in the classroom?

We know that one of the most powerful features of effective homework is the explicit link with classroom learning. If students can see that the homework they do has an impact on their confidence, knowledge and achievement in the classroom, they are more likely to complete it well.

To nudge norms, Peps Mccrea suggests we should amplify desirable behaviours by praising positive individual and group actions (Mccrea, 2020). For instance, instead of focusing on the students who haven't completed their homework, we need to praise those who have and explicitly highlight how this has increased their classroom successes.

'Well done, Sachin, you were able to answer this style of question correctly because of all that work you did on the homework this week!' is far more influential than 'Rishab, you cannot answer this question because you didn't do your homework this week'.

Firstly, you need to have clarity on what you want the norm to *be* in your classroom. To do this, you need to have thought about the ethos of learning in your subject. By not just limiting it to your classroom, you send the message that learning does not just happen in the classroom but is an ongoing process.

Your aim should be achieving effective homework that enhances student confidence, achievement and habit formation. In order to attain this, your ethos should be along the lines of:

> In this subject, we think deeply about our learning by attending to and putting in maximum effort into the tasks we complete.

Therefore, this does not include students who complete homework to avoid a sanction or without thought.

Let us analyse the behaviours this ethos can develop:

- Focus during classroom instruction: to be successful at a task, students need to listen to and comprehend the task instructions.

- Seek clarity: if an aspect of the task is hindering success due to a lack of clarity, a student who is thinking deeply about their learning will seek clarification.

- Seek prompts or support: a motivated student will use all their available resources to succeed at a task.

- Committed completion: instead of the focus being on completion (*I did my homework in 5 minutes*), motivated students will place emphasis on commitment to actively thinking about it (*I thought about the questions I answered on my homework*).

- Building schemata: students who actively think about their homework will be better able to identify links between concepts than those who complete it without thought or those that don't even attempt their homework. This practice elevates students from simply using knowledge towards mastery provided it is thoughtful, varied and spaced (Furst, 2022).

To get to this stage, persistence and positive amplification are key. Let us explore two classroom scenarios:

| Classroom A | Classroom B |
|---|---|
| Ms H starts the term well. Students are set a weekly, short piece of homework and she discusses it regularly in lessons.<br><br>The last couple of weeks of term arrive and there are several disruptions to lessons – students being taken out for choir practice or trips, lessons being used for services and additional assemblies. | Ms E starts the term well. Students are set a weekly, short piece of homework and she discusses it regularly in lessons. She explains the importance of homework to students and provides additional, independent study tasks that students can complete if the usual homework is not set for any reason. These include: look, cover, write, check and retrieval quizzing.<br><br>The last couple of weeks of term arrive and there are several disruptions to lessons – students being taken out for choir practice or trips, lessons being used for services and additional assemblies. |

(*continued*)

| Classroom A | Classroom B |
|---|---|
| Ms H decides not to set homework in the last 2 weeks or during the holiday.<br><br>Students return from the holiday and the break has meant they don't feel overwhelmed with work.<br><br>Ms H restarts the homework routine only to find she is back to square one.<br><br>As the year progresses, more disruptions, illness or planned cover mean that homework is no longer set routinely. | Ms E still sets homework in these last 2 weeks and reminds students that doing a short piece of homework each week means they are still practising their learning and building good habits. She does not set homework during the holidays.<br><br>Students return from the holiday and the break has meant they don't feel overwhelmed with work.<br><br>Ms E restarts the homework routine and finds that a few reminders are needed to get students back into working weekly.<br><br>As the year progresses, more disruptions, illness or planned cover occur but as students have been provided alternate forms of homework, most continue working each week. Ms E praises students who continue to complete independent study and links their efforts with successes in the classroom. |

My own classroom has slowly moved from Classroom A to B over the years. Unexpected (and expected) disruptions do occur throughout the year. Planning for these in advance means that students do not miss out on the benefits of the routine, successes and norms associated with homework completion. Over time, these will help students feel more motivated as they reap the benefits of their efforts.

## How Can Homework Help Students Feel They Belong?

If you had asked me this question years ago, I would have said that it simply cannot. I would have said that surely homework alienates students who don't do it and, more importantly, those who cannot do it.

If we are setting effective, accessible homework then it is a significant contributor to helping our students feel belonging in the classroom. How so? Let us explore a scenario featuring Narender and Sachin.

Narender confidently raised his hand in class, answering yet another question well. His consistent homework and keen attention had made the lesson very easy to follow. In fact, he was able to think ahead and pose questions to make better sense of the topic.

Meanwhile, Sachin slumped in his seat, feeling increasingly disconnected. He had once again forgotten to do his homework and couldn't follow the lesson. His mind wandered, making it even harder to grasp the topic at hand.

The caveat for homework to build feelings of belonging is that students actually spend time thinking about the homework. If Narender did his homework without much thought, simply going through the motion of working, then he wouldn't feel much belonging in the classroom either.

A common argument here is that we could avoid Sachin feeling the way he does if we didn't set homework in the first place. Speaking from personal experience, this is untrue. Students who are motivated to learn and have good study habits will tend to work independently at home whether homework is set or not. Sometimes, these students may not actually *want* to work independently but their parents may organise extra tuition in the form of tutoring sessions so they are continually reviewing work. Some others may be motivated to get better grades and so will work towards achieving these through regular, independent study.

By setting homework, we are providing structure and a chance at building important study habits for our students who are more like Sachin.

## Chapter Summary

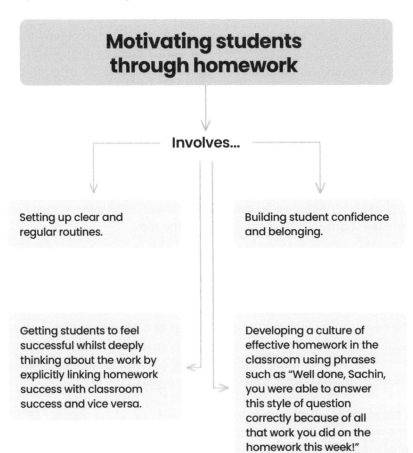

# References

Barron, K. E. and Hulleman, C. S., 2015. Expectancy-value-cost model of motivation. *Psychology*, 84, pp. 261–271.

Bempechat, J., 2019. The case for (quality) homework: Why it improves learning and how parents can help. *Education Next*, 19(1), pp. 36–43.

Furst, E., 2022. *Learning in the brain.* (Online) Available at: https://sites.google.com/view/efratfurst/learning-in-the-brain?pli=1 (Accessed 31 July 2023).

Mccrea, P., 2020. *Motivated Teaching: Harnessing the Science of Motivation to Boost Attention and Effort in the Classroom.* High Impact Teaching.

Ryan, R. M. and Deci, E. L., 2017. Self-determination theory: Basic psychological needs in motivation, development, and wellness. *American Psychologist*, 55(1), pp. 68–78.

Soderstrom, N. C. and Bjork, R. A., 2015. Learning versus performance: An integrative review. *Perspectives on Psychological Science*, 10(2), pp. 176–199.

# 5 The Role of the Home in Successful Homework

In general, students don't like homework - a statement that is hardly revelatory.

Even the students that teachers perceive to be 'good' usually do not rate homework. I remember having a conversation with a student who always got the highest mark in every assessment. I asked them what they thought about homework and why they did it each time without fail. I was trying to better understand what motivated them and, therefore, how I could develop that same motivation in my other students.

As you might have expected, my face fell when they said they did the homework so they didn't get a detention. Definitely not the response I was hoping for.

Acknowledging and understanding parental and student roles is crucial when building a homework culture in schools. With support from both the parents and the student, homework has a greater chance of being effective and benefitting them. This chapter will explore:

- How attitudes can influence the efficacy of homework.
- The roles parents play when it comes to homework.
- How schools can include the home.

DOI: 10.4324/9781003434986-6

## Attitudes

Pierre Bourdieu, a French sociologist, introduced the concept of 'habitus', which he defined as a set of dispositions, attitudes and behaviours that are developed through upbringing, social class and experiences. An individual's perception of the world and their actions are influenced by these dispositions (Nash, 1990).

Students can bring different sets of habitus to schools. This can manifest as varied attitudes towards education, expectations of success and ways of interacting with schools. This undoubtedly plays a significant role in whether students value homework.

It raises a key question for us to consider: Does a student's habitus align with the academic expectations and ethos of the school?

For example, a student may have low expectations of success due to past history or a lack of confidence. They will struggle to think positively about homework as they may not see the point – they are not going to succeed anyway.

A further consideration is the parents' own habitus, which can affect their expectations for their children. This, in turn, influences the type and level of support or pressure they provide concerning homework.

I grew up in an environment where students were expected to excel and if you didn't achieve the highest possible mark, you were considered a failure. I was lucky as my own parents never placed this pressure on me but I vividly remember a classmate asking me *not* to do well on an upcoming assessment so she could do better than me and her parents would be happy with her achievements.

Much like we have seen in Chapter 2 about how what we know influences what we learn, a student's and parent's habitus can impact *what* they acquire from homework and *how* this is achieved.

Homework can act as a barrier to educational success and social mobility if the family habitus does not equip students with the skills, resources or, crucially, the right attitudes needed to complete it effectively.

Let us consider two family scenarios:

| Family A | Family B |
| --- | --- |
| Daisy is being raised by a single mother who has two jobs. | Dorothy's dad is away a lot because of his job, whilst her mum works from home. Dorothy is usually late to school because she misses her alarm and is slow to get ready. |
| Daisy has to drop off and pick up her two younger siblings from nursery and primary school every day. She is usually late to school herself and gets a late mark each time. | She struggles to complete much homework because she just isn't motivated to do it and feels it is a waste of time. |
| She struggles to complete too much homework but does try to do as much as she can. | Her mum asks her if she has done her homework to which she always says 'yes' even when this is not true. |
| She can never stay back after school for detention or clubs because there is no one else who can pick up or look after her younger siblings. | Dorothy usually finds herself in detention after school, which she doesn't mind because her friends are usually in detention too. |
| When Daisy gets home, she has to cook tea and wash up. She can only work on her homework once her siblings are in bed. Her mum always asks about her school work and encourages her to complete as much homework as possible, discussing why it is important regularly. | When Dorothy brings home assessments and has not achieved well, her parents ask about it, say that it is not good enough and tell her to do more work. In turn, Dorothy spends more time on the computer, telling her parents she is revising, but in reality, is getting distracted watching videos. |
| When Daisy brings home assessments, her mum sits with her (when she can) to see where she did well and how she could have improved. | |

Both Daisy and Dorothy struggle to complete homework for different reasons.

With Daisy, her situation means she does not have enough time to complete many pieces of homework to a high standard. Several family commitments compete for her attention. Her mother is supportive and encouraging, which spurs Daisy on to complete as much work as possible. But is 'what is possible' enough in the eyes of the school? Does the school's expectations and values align with the amount of work Daisy is able to do?

From the school's perspective, it may be easy to cut Daisy some slack and say that she doesn't have to complete all the pieces of work. But let's assume that Dorothy is in the same class as Daisy. Whilst Dorothy may get a detention for not completing homework, Daisy is let off.

Both students are getting mixed messages about what is important and what is acceptable by the school and, indeed, will develop their habitus further.

For Daisy, her sense of success will be lower and this, in turn, will lower her own expectations and value of the work she is doing independently. For Dorothy, it will further lower her own expectations of success because when she completes the same level of work as her peers, she is penalised for it.

Parental attitudes in both cases are important to consider and acknowledge.

In both cases, the parental figure is busy and hardworking. Both sets of parents find it difficult to be fully involved in their child's independent study. Their own habitus can significantly influence the development of their child's habitus – Did they value homework when they were younger? Did their efforts pay off and so they believe in effortful thinking being a key factor in academic success?

With Daisy's mother, the importance she assigns to education permeates the conversations she has with her daughter. She acknowledges the value of homework, discusses academic achievements regularly and supports Daisy in achieving well despite being busy with work.

With Dorothy's parents, whilst some discussion about academic achievements does take place, their influence and guidance in how to improve is minimal – they tell their daughter *what* she has to do (work more) but not support her with *how* to achieve this (Dorothy spends more time on the computer). This may be because they want to provide more autonomous support and allow Dorothy to take the lead in her own study. How do parents decide what level of autonomy to grant their child during independent study?

## Parental Roles

Hoover-Dempsey et al. have explored and identified several strategies that parents can employ to get involved in their children's homework and independent study (Hoover-Dempsey, 2001). They argue that the effectiveness of parental involvement depends on the alignment between the school's values and the parents' assistance, the student's perception of parental involvement and the specific strategies employed by the parents.

Unsurprisingly, when parents emphasise mastery and aim for their child to achieve it, the child is more likely to aim for mastery as well (Madjar, 2016). But this effect is an indirect one and is only significant when parents provide support in the form of autonomy and a belief in their child's success (Gonida, 2014).

Let's look at the main strategies (Hoover-Dempsey, 2001) that parents can employ:

### *Establishing Physical and Psychological Structures for the Child's Homework Performance*

Students are more likely to succeed at their homework if working in an environment conducive to learning. Parents can support with the right physical and psychological environment by ensuring their child can work in a space with the right lighting, noise level and limited access to distractions (such as the television). They can support by having an ethos of assigning importance to homework completion and valuing the benefits completion will have on the academic and overall development of their child.

### Interacting With the Student's School or Teacher About Homework

If parents know the type and frequency of homework to expect, they are in a better position to help their child with achieving success. Communication with the school should be straightforward to enable supportive parental involvement.

As the mother to two primary-aged children, I find it helpful to receive a fortnightly letter with short tasks that my children are expected to complete. As a secondary school teacher, in place of regular emails and letters, I set the same style of homework on the same day each week so students and parents become familiar with the format and frequency of tasks.

### Providing a General Oversight of the Homework Process

Having an oversight of the homework process includes seeking help from external sources such as hiring a tutor or buying resources such as revision guides. In addition, parents may employ either intrusive or supportive strategies when being involved with their child's homework.

Intrusive strategies would include providing a rigid schedule and structure around homework completion and potentially unwarranted interruptions. These types of strategies may contribute to their child becoming dependent and, possibly, helpless when it comes to independent study (Orkin, 2017). Supportive strategies would include asking about the homework but allowing their child to have ownership of their schedule and work process.

The judgement parents have to make with regard to whether they should be supportive or intrusive is a difficult one. The variation in strategies employed depends on several factors including their child's motivation, self-efficacy and self-regulation.

For instance, my son requires more intrusive strategies in order to succeed at his homework as he has not yet fully developed self-regulation practices but the level of direct control is lower than it was a couple of years ago when he started getting homework.

## Responding to the Student's Homework Performance

Praise and/or criticism are significant levers in homework parental support and can influence student motivation. If parents promise an extrinsic reward such as a treat for homework completion, their child will more likely achieve short-term success but the long-term benefits of homework can be impacted (as there are only so many rewards one can offer).

How parents respond to homework performance and completion can develop their child's habitus. For instance, if parents expect a certain standard of performance (e.g. not minimal, thought and effort are the norm), their child will associate learning with effort and reaching a standard. If, on the other hand, parents expect an hour spent on homework without monitoring what takes place within that hour, their child will associate learning with time spent on it regardless of how much thinking has taken place in that time.

## Engaging in Homework Processes and Tasks with the Student

Parental support with the tasks can range from content-driven to autonomous, with the latter being associated with better student outcomes (Gonida, 2014).

When parents provide content-driven support, they may engage in strategies including sitting with their child whilst they complete homework, checking each step that is attempted and assisting with or even doing the homework themselves.

Whereas, autonomous support would involve parents showing an interest, providing encouragement and regular check-ins whilst their child complete homework.

Support can be difficult to provide if parents do not feel they know or understand a school's homework practices. This is particularly true as students progress from primary to secondary education in the UK, where parents may feel less confident with helping with difficult subject content or unclear homework practices (Hallam, 2009).

### Engaging in Meta-Strategies That Help the Student Learn Processes Conducive to Achievement

At its heart, meta-strategies involve teaching students how to learn, fostering a deep understanding of the learning process itself. Teachers can encourage students to reflect on their own learning strategies and adjust them as needed.

Encouraging self-regulation, time management and goal setting empowers students to take control of their own learning. In doing so, they develop essential lifelong study habits.

Parents can play a crucial role by instilling these meta-strategies and providing a supportive environment for their child's academic growth. Initially, this may be in the form of direct input and guidance in creating a schedule for independent study and removing distractions. Eventually, this would evolve into more autonomous support and discussions of how the time spent studying was spent.

In addition, two further strategies were described by Hoover-Dempsey et al. that parents can employ to support children. However, these strategies assume the role of the teacher and are therefore not beneficial when considering parental involvement in successful homework. These are detailed below.

### Engaging in Meta-Strategies Designed to Create a Fit Between the Task and Student Skill Levels

In some cases, parents can further support their child by breaking the tasks into manageable chunks and checking the progress of each. Whilst this may be necessary for younger primary-aged children, homework is most effective when the teacher determines the manageable tasks that students must complete. This is important because it is the teacher who has a greater understanding of the task and the role of that task in developing learning. Whilst parents may have an idea, it should not be up to them to determine how best to fit the task to their child's skill levels.

### Engaging in Interactive Processes Supporting Student Understanding of Homework

Parents can support student understanding by asking questions about the task and its purpose in developing their child's learning. In addition, as previously mentioned, they may provide a supportive environment and resources that can help their child succeed at the homework.

Teachers can support parents by providing an overview of the purpose of the homework task and how it will benefit their child. This, in turn, will help parents provide the right encouragement for their child to put in effort and complete their homework and ask the right questions to check that the homework has had its intended impact.

## What Can Schools Do?

Students whose habitus is aligned with the dominant culture within schools often find it easier to complete homework, thereby reinforcing their social advantages. If the habitus of their parents are also aligned, then the chance of the homework being effective is significantly increased.

The aim of a school in developing a successful homework culture would be to align the values of the student, parent and school (Figure 5.1). This is no easy feat.

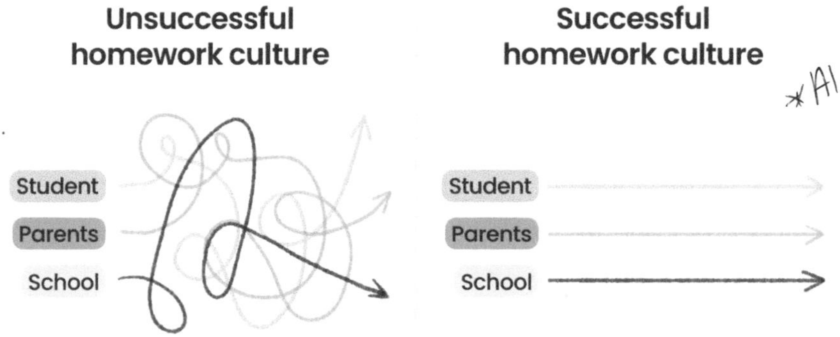

**Unsuccessful homework culture**

**Successful homework culture**

ha!

\* Alignment (Biggs)

Student

Parents

School

Student

Parents

School

Figure 5.1 In an unsuccessful homework culture, the views of students, parents and the school are misaligned. A successful homework culture enables all stakeholders to have the same goal.

Firstly, we need to understand that parents may sometimes view homework negatively due to the following reasons (Xu, 2003):

- It is a source of tension at home where parents and their child may clash over whether the latter has any homework and if they have completed it.

- They are unsure how to help their child.

- They feel excluded from the whole process.

- They do not value homework, either in general or due to the particular nature of the homework being set. This can cause conflict due to having to support something they do not believe in.

So it seems schools have a lot to consider to make homework successful. Firstly, the homework itself needs to be effective. It should encourage effortful thinking from the students completing it and they need to see themselves being successful at the task. This will develop their habitus, as they see the homework as something they can access and at which they can expect to succeed. Ensuring the rewards in terms of confidence in the classroom and academic achievements are explicitly demonstrated to students further increases the efficacy of the homework (see Chapter 3 for more on this).

## What Can Schools Do About Parental Attitudes and Support?

Schools can implement a three-pronged approach to involve parents and assist them in encouraging and supporting their child.

*Ensure access and Task Instructions are Clear for Both Parents and Students to Follow*

Consider the two sets of instructions to complete the same task:

SET A

Write a report in the style we did in class on 'The effect of smoking on lung function'. Your report should be no longer than one page of your exercise book (one side of an A4 sheet). Use BBC Bitesize to help if stuck.

SET B

Write a report on 'The effect of smoking on lung function'. Your report should be no longer than one page of your exercise book (one side of an A4 sheet) and should have the following:

- How the lung normally functions (mention the path air takes to enter and leave the lungs and how the alveoli work).

- What is contained in cigarette smoke?

- The effects of each component of cigarette smoke on the path of air and alveoli function.

*Resources to use:*

- Model answer in your exercise book and the online sharing platform.

- BBC Bitesize (search within KS3 for lung function, alveoli and cigarette smoke).

The instructions in Set B are not only clear for the student, especially if they have missed any recent lessons, but also support the parent in knowing exactly what to do and where to look for help. With Set A, a parent who may not be quite familiar with the content or the format and style used in lessons would feel less empowered to support their child with the homework.

## Communicate The School's Approach to Homework

Organise information booklets, information evenings, live online sessions, pre-recorded sessions, letters and sections on the school website to vary the means of communication you provide to parents so they know the purpose, types and frequency of homework to expect for different subjects. An example of these means of communication is provided in Chapter 9.

Parents who understand *why* homework is being set and *how* the format, frequency and type represent this purpose will be more inclined to support and value the school's homework implementation. In addition, schools should also communicate how parents can help and the school's expectations. Should they sit with their child when they complete the homework? Should they check the work before submission? Should they be involved in quizzing their child? If the answer is yes to the latter, how can the questions be accessed? How often should they quiz their child?

For my primary-aged children, my direct involvement is certainly higher than my own expectations of the parents of my secondary-aged students. Indeed, my children's primary school asks us to quiz, check and encourage them with their homework.

## Inform Parents of How Their Child is Doing in Terms of Homework

The first time a student struggles with homework, contact home to inform them and discuss how their child can be supported. If they couldn't access the homework, how can the school ensure this will no longer be an issue? If they forgot to do the homework, how can the school work with the parent to help the student organise their time better? If they were not motivated to do the homework, how can the school and parent work together to encourage the student to work at the task in the future?

Through reports and reward systems, ensure parents also know when their child is succeeding at the homework - either completing it each time or doing a good job. See Chapter 7 for more on rewards and sanctions.

## Chapter Summary

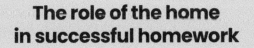

**The role of the home in successful homework**

Involves...

Attitudes that align with the school ethos whereby both see the value in regular and manageable homework.

Providing the right physical and psychological space for students to work in.

Taking a proactive and supportive approach over the homework process and performance by providing resources or support, discussions about homework completion, performance and impact.

Communication with the school to minimise barriers and augment support, which is a two-way process as parents should be able to ask for help, clarification or support. Schools explain the purpose, format, type and frequency of homework and regularly inform parents of how their child is faring.

## References

Gonida, E. N. and Cortina, K. S., 2014. Parental involvement in homework: Relations with parent and student achievement-related motivational beliefs and achievement. *British Journal of Education Psychology*, 84, pp. 376-396.

Hallam, S., 2009. Parents' perspectives on homework: United Kingdom, New Zealand, and Japan. In: R. Deslandes, ed. *International Perspectives on Student Outcomes and Homework: Family-School-Community Partnerships*. London: Routledge, p. 47.

Hoover-Dempsey, K. V., Battiato, A. C., Walker, J. M. T., Reed, R. P., DeJong, J. M. and Jones, K. P., 2001. Parental involvement in homework. *Educational Psychologist*, 36(3), pp. 195-209.

Madjar, N., Shklar, N. and Moshe, L., 2016. The role of parental attitudes in children's motivation towards homework assignments. *Psychology in the Schools*, 53(2), pp. 173-188.

Nash, R., 1990. Bourdieu on education and social and cultural reproduction. *British Journal of Sociology of Education*, 11(4), pp. 431-447.

Orkin, M., May, S. and Wolf, M., 2017. How parental support during homework contributes to helpless behaviours among struggling readers. *Reading Psychology*, 38, pp. 506-541.

Xu, J. and Yuan, R., 2003. Doing homework: Listening to students,' parents,' and teachers' voices in one urban middle school community. *School Community Journal*, 13(2), p. 25.

# 6 Supporting Students With Homework

We now know:

- Why we should be discussing homework.

- What the research says about how we learn.

- What makes the homework effective.

- How motivation works and the role homework can play in this.

- The role of the home in making homework effective.

One aspect that is notably lacking in research on homework is the role of the student. A lot of emphasis is on the school, teachers, circumstances and parents. In the previous chapter, we briefly looked at student attitudes and habitus and how this can influence whether homework is effective or not. In this chapter, we will further explore the student's perspective and how teachers can support students to build lifelong habits associated with homework.

## The Role of the Student

In Chapter 4, we looked at the range of steps a student needed to follow to be successful at doing their homework. These steps are repeated here:

- Organise their time.

- Prepare a place to work quietly.

DOI: 10.4324/9781003434986-7

- Turn off devices or move away from things that may distract.

- Access the homework, e.g. a worksheet that wasn't stuck in or inputting their password correctly.

- Read the instructions carefully.

- Complete all the parts of the homework.

- Think about the homework whilst working on it.

- Submit the homework or stick the sheet in their book.

We expect rather a lot from students each time we set them homework. In some cases, supporting students with similar steps in the classroom is hard enough – How do we support them when they are away from our direct influence?

There are two factors that are key: habits and belief.

### Which Comes First: Habits or Belief?

When I first started to teach, I didn't quite know how to organise my time or what was the most efficient way to plan lessons. I would spend hours on lesson plans and resources for each lesson, sometimes preparing several different worksheets for the same lesson. I found it really difficult to get into a habit of planning efficiently and thinking about my practice until I observed other teachers, got more confident with the subject content and read many articles on teaching. I mimicked some of the habits and routines that other, successful teachers followed, felt more sure of my subject knowledge and only then did my own planning improve.

It is very similar for our students. For them to get into the right habits, they need to feel that they can actually accomplish something and be successful at it. But to have an expectation of success, the right habits help. The more routinely students work at something, the more they grow in confidence, which then helps them stick to the routine.

### *Supporting Students With the Steps Involved in Successful Homework*

We have now seen that there are three stakeholders when it comes to homework: the student, the teacher and the parent. Amongst the myriad steps required for students to excel in their homework, a collaborative effort amongst these three stakeholders is instrumental in providing the necessary support. Table 6.1 explores each step, how each stakeholder can provide support and why that support is important.

## The Student's Perspective

### *Motivation*

Some students have said to me that they will only work for a teacher they like. In the past, this has prompted me to try and make my lessons fun and engaging and going so far as to set fun and engaging homework tasks as well. But if we delve deeper into that first sentence, we may begin to understand what inspires a student to 'work'.

Motivational theory tells us that students (and indeed everyone) will feel far more motivated to do something if they feel belonging. For a student entering a classroom, where their habitus suggests they will likely not succeed, either at knowing any answers, making links between concepts or at behaving well, they will probably *not* feel a sense of belonging.

Now, if that student is given homework during the lesson, they will feel less inclined to want to complete it, or if they do, they may be motivated by avoiding a sanction rather than enhancing their learning.

We need to ensure students feel that they have a firm place within the classroom learning environment – a place in which they can thrive and succeed, where they can interact with others who share the same sense of belonging.

So when students say they only work for teachers they like, they may *think* it is because the teacher makes them laugh or because there is a

Table 6.1 A series of tables discussing the various ways in which students, parents and teachers can support students at different steps involved in homework.

**Step: organise their time**

| Where does the support come from? | How is the support given? | Why is this important? |
|---|---|---|
| Student | • Create a timetable to plan what homework tasks to work on in a day, including how long each task will take.<br>• Ensure homework is completed earlier in the evening rather than late at night, just before bed. | A student could very quickly feel overwhelmed with all the tasks they have to complete each day, including chores, family commitments and extracurricular activities. Having a clear plan means students are less likely to forget to do a piece of homework and are therefore more likely to succeed. |
| Parent | • Help the child with making the timetable.<br>• Ensure other activities do not clash or impact the timetable often. | |

*(continued)*

# amazon.co.uk®

A gift from **Jo Castelino**

*Hi Carl, I hope you like my book! From Jo Castelino*

Gift note included with **The Homework Conundrum: How to Stop the Dog From Eating Homework (The Teacher CPD Academy)**

*Table 6.1* (continued)

**Step: prepare a place to work quietly and move away from distractions**

| Where does the support come from? | How is the support given? | Why is this important? |
|---|---|---|
| Student | • Ensure homework is done at a desk or table and not on the bed.<br>• Turn off TV, radio, phone or any other device. | Whilst calming, relaxing music has been shown to improve performance on memory tasks (Hallam, 2002), music that is arousing or includes lyrics takes attention away from the task at hand, if the task is complex (Gonzalez, 2019). |
| Parent | • Help their child by minimising access to distracting devices and noisy areas.<br>• Ensure there is a flat surface for their child to work on. | When students work on a flat surface there are obvious advantages such as arranging resources like books and calculators in an accessible place rather than on bed covers. However, a further advantage to working at a desk rather than the bed is the demarcation of leisure and study. |

(continued)

*Table 6.1* (continued)

**Step: access the homework**

| Where does the support come from? | How is the support given? | Why is this important? |
|---|---|---|
| Student | • Make an effort to access the homework whether it is online or on a sheet.<br>• Ask for help if they are unsure about how to access homework.<br>• Use the right resources to help with the task. | In order for students to successfully access homework, we need to consider both physical and mental access. Do students and parents know where to find helpful resources such as notes and explanations? Are these readily available? Do they know how to use these resources in order to maximise success?<br><br>Are students familiar with the task? Do they know what they can do if they are stuck? |
| Parent | • Inform the teacher on behalf of their child if access is difficult due to poor internet connectivity or other reasons.<br>• Ensure the right resources are available. | |
| Teacher | • Ensure resources are easily available for students, especially if they are needed in order to be successful at the homework.<br>• Practise similar tasks in the classroom so students know exactly what they are required to do. | |

*(continued)*

*Table 6.1* (continued)

**Step: read and follow instructions carefully**

| Where does the support come from? | How is the support given? | Why is this important? |
|---|---|---|
| Student | • Check the instructions and flag any that don't make sense or that are confusing.<br>• Check back on instructions so they are sure they have followed all steps. | In my experience, students tend to give up more easily if instructions either do not make sense or are too complicated and unfamiliar. There is one potential disadvantage to familiarity, however. If students develop a habit with completing a piece of homework where they do not follow all steps properly, then it is harder to get students to break out of poor habits. Ensuring there is practice and checks that students are following all steps correctly will minimise issues related to familiarity. |
| Teacher | • Go through the instructions in the classroom so students know exactly what to do.<br>• Provide hints or exemplars so students know what the product should look like.<br>• Practice identical steps in the classroom so students are aware of how to check they have successfully completed all parts of the task. | |

(continued)

*Table 6.1* (continued)

| Step: think about the task whilst completing homework | | |
|---|---|---|
| **Where does the support come from?** | **How is the support given?** | **Why is this important?** |
| Student | • Focus on the task at hand and refrain from thinking about anything unrelated to the task. | It is easy to drift when working on something. Whilst I have been working on this book, I have paused a number of times where my thought process has turned to something completely irrelevant. We cannot control every thought our students have, nor should we but it our duty to show students how to complete a task that we have designed to improve their learning. What can our students do when it is hard to focus? |
| Teacher | • Practise tasks and conditions similar to the homework so students know what is expected of them to be successful at the homework. | Research tells us that taking time for themselves, eating well including at breakfast and getting enough sleep are important factors in ensuring students don't procrastinate and lose focus. Indeed, getting enough sleep is key to the learning process and helps students remember more in the long term (InnerDrive, n.d.) |

(continued)

*Table 6.1* (continued)

**Step: submit the homework**

| Where does the support come from? | How is the support given? | Why is this important? |
|---|---|---|
| Student | • Submit the piece of homework in the way expected by the teacher.<br>• Contact the teacher if there are any issues with submission. | Echoing the importance of following instructions, students need to follow the right procedure to submit their homework so teachers can feed back on it effectively. |

fun activity. In reality, students feel like they belong when they know the learning is achievable and they are a part of a community in the classroom (Keyes, 2019).

In order to foster this sense of belonging, teachers need to have clear and consistent routines in place. If students know what to expect and 'how something is done in this classroom', they can seamlessly fit in within that classroom.

### Does Homework Further Disadvantage the Disadvantaged?

A common objection people have to homework is that it disadvantages the already disadvantaged. In fact, it has been said that homework may penalise those who come from low-income backgrounds because they may not have the same access to resources, a quiet space at home to work in or the lack of time parents may have to assist their child (O'Keeffe, 2023). It has also been said that parents from low-income families may not be as highly educated as parents from higher-income families or they may not understand the language as well. All of these purported reasons imply these parents cannot or will not support their child with homework in the same way as parents from affluent families (Bempechat, 2019).

However, research shows us that families from disadvantaged backgrounds are far from absent, uninterested or deficient in supporting their children with homework and school work – instead, they value education and attempt various ways of supporting their children through providing resources and encouragement (De Luigi, 2015).

Indeed, our *perceptions* of whether students from disadvantaged backgrounds can access or complete homework or if the parents of these students value or can support their child can further perpetuate their disadvantage. These perceptions and biases can manifest themselves through our words and actions – whether we expect parental involvement in supporting homework or if we expect students from disadvantaged backgrounds to complete homework to the same level as those from affluent backgrounds (Felix, 2008).

### *If I Am Working for Hours in the Classroom, Why Am I Expected to Work Outside of It Too?*

A further objection to homework raised by students, parents and some teachers is that if we are expecting students to work in the classroom for hours, why are we expecting more work outside of the classroom? Why can't teachers complete all the work required of students during school hours and not outside of them? Doesn't this suggest the work we are covering is not of a good standard if further work is required beyond the classroom? We don't expect most other professions to carry on working once they are home from work so why do we have these expectations for our students (obviously we are not including teaching in this last objection!)?

All of these objections are understandable and on the face of it, they seem reasonable. But there are counterarguments for these objections.

The key caveat here is that the homework is effective and is based on how learning happens rather than being a means to complete unfinished tasks or independently explore new concepts.

This change in mindset is necessary to gauge the purpose and importance of homework. If our goal is to foster confidence, lifelong habits of independent study and academic achievement, then homework is an important extension of classroom learning.

All the learning taking place in the classroom is under the direct guidance of the teacher. If our students are struggling, we are right there to help them. We provide immediate feedback on things they get right and things they need to improve on. We provide immediate feedback when they are not focused on the task at hand. We control the fact that they cannot just stand up and eat a snack during the lesson because it isn't break time yet.

As students progress through school, our expectations of how much independent study takes place increase. By the time they are ready to complete their General Certificate of Secondary Education (GCSE) exams, we expect our students to revise by themselves, away from our direct influence.

It is unrealistic to expect students to seamlessly transition the habits cultivated under our tutelage in the classroom to a home setting in Year 11, devoid of our direct support. Not unless we build on the practice of these skills through structured, regular homework.

## How Can Schools Support Students?

Schools play an important role in creating a good environment for students to do their homework. By having a well-organised plan, schools can facilitate a seamless transition between learning in the classroom and working independently at home. As discussed before, a collaborative effort involving parents, teachers and the student is key.

Teachers can give clear instructions, build routines and provide resources and feedback (Chapter 3), whilst parents can make sure there's a supportive setting at home for doing homework (Chapter 5).

What can schools, as a whole, do? For the main part, the school is the place where the culture of doing homework is built and maintained (more in Chapter 8).

There are some steps schools can take to provide students with tangible support.

### Physical Access

Students' access to resources and the homework task is a critical factor that influences their ability to complete homework effectively.

Schools can set up an online sharing platform such as Google Classroom or Microsoft Teams, so students and parents can always access worksheets and online resources that may be required for the successful completion of homework.

If internet connectivity and devices are lacking, easy access to physical copies of the homework in the form of a booklet or sheets is important.

Schools must check that access is not an issue for students through making expectations clear in advance. For example, if a teacher is planning to set an online homework, check that all students can access the internet with no issues for the duration of the homework. Teachers should be mindful of the fact that not all students are aware of or comfortable with informing the teacher of a lack of device or internet connectivity. A suggestion here would be to contact home directly to explain the expectations and find out if there are any access issues.

## Organisation

Students often find themselves juggling a multitude of responsibilities, such as packing the right books, ensuring they bring in the right equipment to school and completing homework. The latter task not only requires organisation but a lot of attention too. It is no wonder some of our students struggle with completing these responsibilities and succeeding at them.

The struggle with organisation often stems from a lack of experience or underdeveloped time-management skills. This challenge is exacerbated when homework from different subjects starts to pile up, each with their own deadline and set of requirements. Without a well-structured approach, students can easily become overwhelmed, leading to procrastination, missed deadlines, lacklustre effort and underperformance. The need for support in developing organisational skills is paramount, as it not only aids in managing the process of homework but also instils a sense of self-discipline.

As teachers, several of us use either a physical or an online planner to help us remember all the tasks we are expected to complete, the deadlines we need to meet and the finer detail of achieving each task successfully.

A student planner with space for students to record each piece of homework, any details that will help them complete it well and the date it is due is a useful piece of equipment. Some schools provide homework booklets with pre-recorded tasks and deadlines that have a lot of the organisational element simplified for students. One disadvantage of this latter option is some of the responsiveness of homework is minimised. As we have seen in Chapter 3, responsive homework is most effective because the homework task is tailored to the student's learning needs. If a student has already mastered something and then is given homework to practise it further, the efficacy of that homework is significantly compromised. There are no gains to be made here and the student will most likely lose interest and not spent time deeply thinking about the task.

Simply providing a student planner or homework booklet is not enough to help our students organise themselves and develop the right habits and self-discipline. They need to be explicitly taught how to use these resources well and this use needs to be monitored over time with regular check-ins and support.

Schools can also help students organise themselves with visual and verbal reminders of homework task deadlines and expectations. This can be in the form of a Homework Board that is on display as well as a quick reminder by teachers that the homework is due the following lesson.

Providing as much support with these aspects of organisation does not disempower our students or prevent them from developing good independent study habits. Our aim is to help our students develop good habits when it comes to removing distractions and thinking deeply about the homework. Any support we provide with the other aspects of homework will give our students every chance of success.

## Time

When students are given several pieces of homework from different subjects, the demands of the multiple tasks, varying levels of difficulty and extracurricular activities have the potential to create a stressful environment. Schools can play a pivotal role in aiding students with time management.

One suggestion would be for teachers to distribute the workload evenly over the week, preventing the clustering of deadlines, which can overwhelm students. However, this would require monumental coordination and pre-planning, which is not always feasible in schools. A certain understanding and discussion amongst teachers of subjects that do not see their students often will have less flexibility over when they set their homework, whereas teachers of subjects that are core (such as English) can coordinate with others to ensure their homework deadline does not regularly clash with several other deadlines.

Additionally, integrating technology such as homework management apps can help students track assignments and manage their time better. Microsoft Teams, Google Classroom and Satchel One are some examples of online platforms that can provide reminders to students about upcoming deadlines.

There should also be due consideration of the amount and regularity of homework in the Homework Policy that is then shared and communicated with all stakeholders (see an example in Chapter 9).

Some students struggle with homework due to family commitments or extracurricular activities. Providing opportunities for students to work on their homework in school means they are given chances to succeed. Schools can run homework clubs at lunchtime or after-school (or both) as well as support sessions that students can opt into so they can practise accessing the homework or asking questions to clarify the task. Homework clubs can also provide students with access to the Internet, if this is a barrier preventing them from successfully completing homework.

## Motivation and Recognition

One of the key aspects of effective homework is recognition of student efforts.

Students may feel demotivated during homework if they do not understand the task or do not receive recognition for their efforts. Schools can significantly ameliorate this by developing a system of recognition and rewards that acknowledge students' achievements and progress. By celebrating successes and providing positive feedback, schools can help students gain in confidence, which, in turn, can enhance their motivation to engage with homework. This does not mean applauding students each time for completing a piece of homework. It means acknowledging that homework completion and a good amount of thought have immediate and delayed benefits that improve student confidence and achievement. It means building a culture where students feel that doing their homework is worth it because when they work at it, this is recognised and appreciated. Moreover, creating a culture where effort and improvement are valued over only appreciating the end result can encourage students to persevere through challenging tasks.

There is great power in feedback that guides students on how to improve, thereby giving them a sense of direction and a measure of control over their own learning process. Through these measures, the cycle of success, recognition and increased self-confidence can significantly boost students' motivation, making the completion of homework a more positive and self-reinforcing experience.

## Chapter Summary

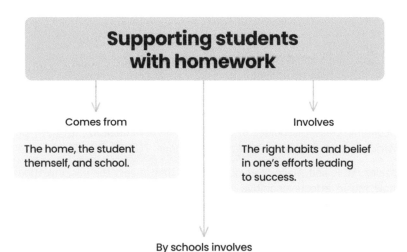

**Supporting students with homework**

**Comes from**

The home, the student themself, and school.

**Involves**

The right habits and belief in one's efforts leading to success.

**By schools involves**

Providing access to the right resources necessary for success, ensuring organisation is feasible and not complicated, building a feeling of belonging as homework is inherently linked to classroom learning and responding to the needs and efforts of students.

## References

Bempechat, J., 2019. The case for (quality) homework: Why it improves learning and how parents can help. *Education Next*, 19(1), pp. 36–43.

De Luigi, N. and Martelli, A., 2015. Attitudes and practices of parents: Disadvantage and access to education access to education. *European Education*, 47, pp. 46–60.

Felix, N., Dornbrack, J. and Scheckle, E., 2008. Parents, homework and socio-economic class: Discourses of deficit and disadvantage in the "new" South Africa. *English Teaching: Practice and Critique*, 7(2), pp. 99–112.

Gonzalez, M. F. and Aiello, J. R., 2019. More than meets the ear: Investigating how music affects cognitive task performance. *Journal of Experimental Psychology: Applied*, 25(3), pp. 431–444.

Hallam, S., Price, J. and Katsarou, G., 2002. The effects of background music on primary school pupils' task performance. *Educational Studies*, 28(2), pp. 111–122.

InnerDrive, n.d. *5 things students need to know to do well in exams.* (Online) Available at: https://blog.innerdrive.co.uk/5-ways-to-do-well-in-exams (Accessed October 2023).

Keyes, T. S., 2019. A qualitative inquiry: Factors that promote classroom belonging and engagement among high school students. *School Community Journal*, 29(1), pp. 171–200.

O'Keeffe, L., Clarke, C., McDonald, S. and Comber, B., 2023. Mathematics homework and the potential compounding of educational disadvantage. *British Journal of Sociology of Education*, 42(2), pp. 1–17.

# 7 Rewards and Sanctions

I distinctly remember two instances from my childhood when it comes to homework:

I had a few pages of maths homework to complete, and I remember sacrificing watching an episode of *Scooby-Doo* (I loved it back then!) to sit down and complete my homework. I remember not minding because I enjoyed the practice – I knew exactly how to complete the problems. There were a few that challenged me, but I enjoyed that and felt proud of the fact that my teacher felt we could solve the tricky sums. Although in my school, we didn't have any rewards, I felt rewarded, especially when I got the highest score in my assessment and felt confident enough to explain the concepts to my peers.

There are a few things that contributed to my feeling of success:

- I understood the content being taught in lessons (this was mainly due to clear explanations).
- My teacher narrated his thinking through his explanations and when going through examples.
- We practised lots of questions in lessons with immediate feedback as to how I was doing.
- The homework was similar to the questions we practised in class.
- The homework was always checked with feedback being given and explanations of how to answer the challenging questions.

DOI: 10.4324/9781003434986-8

I also remember a second instance when it came to my physics homework. I struggled to understand what was going on in lessons. I listened carefully and genuinely tried my best but I simply struggled to understand what we were learning. When it came to the homework, I would sit down and attempt it but have no idea at all. I did not ask my teacher for help, mostly because I was terrified of him. When it came to the homework deadline, the teacher instructed those of us who didn't complete their homework to stand during the lesson so he could berate us. We didn't have detentions, but we were also given what he termed 'imposition' where we wrote the same sentence over and over again and submitted this by the following day.

Unsurprisingly, it is the latter memory that is clearer in my head because of the utter shame I felt.

There are a few things that contributed to my feeling of failure:

- I did not understand the content being taught in lessons (the explanations were not followed by any checks for understanding).

- We used textbooks and simply read from them to 'understand' how to answer questions.

- We practised some questions in lessons but without clear explanations and narration of how to answer them, I struggled in class.

- Homework was on questions I did not understand. Nearly all seemed too challenging for me.

- The punishment only served to embarrass and upset me, instead of motivating me to complete future pieces of homework or feel brave enough to ask for help.

Schools have various forms of rewarding and sanctioning students, with most focused on behaviours within the classroom. However, whilst my school did not have achievement points, reward trips, stickers or detentions, I still felt rewarded or sanctioned if I did my homework or not. Rewards and sanctions, therefore, may not just assume an extrinsic, visible form but may also encompass the feeling induced in the student.

## Rewards

Rewards in the classroom serve as a form of positive reinforcement to encourage desirable behaviours amongst our students. They assume a number of forms such as verbal praise, achievement points, certificates, trophies or even items like stickers, prizes or sweets.

They work by creating a positive and motivating environment, where students are recognised and valued for their efforts and accomplishments. When used effectively, rewards can boost self-esteem, foster a love for learning and promote a positive classroom culture.

### *Role of Rewards*

A good reward shows our students that we appreciate their efforts and know they have done something worthy of praise and recognition. Interestingly, a reward is most effective when it is unexpected (Lepper, 1973). When students expect a reward for something they do, they do not work as much on the task as if they are unaware of a potential reward at the end of the task.

In his book, *Running the Room*, Tom Bennett warns us that rewarding students for expected behaviour desensitises them to the point where they behave in a certain way *only* to receive the reward (Bennett, 2020). The best way to ensure rewards have an effect is to give them out infrequently and only for behaviours that go beyond our basic expectations.

### *Why Do Rewards Work?*

At my previous school, we had Staff Star every Friday, where colleagues could nominate each other for a bit of praise. I was grateful to have received a few in the 6 years I worked there, and each time I did, I felt proud and it set me up for the rest of the day knowing that my colleagues appreciated something I'd done.

We have all seen the transformation in our students when we genuinely praise them for their effort, progress or achievement. This is the result of the praise we provide for work done in the classroom, where we are present to support, encourage and minimise distractions. Praise given to students who do their homework, then, would be even more happily received because that praise is not only for the completion of the homework task but also for managing their time and attention.

Importantly, rewards help us nudge norms in the classroom. Compare the two classrooms as follows:

| Classroom A | Classroom B |
|---|---|
| Ms E has marked a class set of homework and sees them the following lesson. She says well done to those who have done their homework and gives out achievement points to all students who have completed their homework. She knows that Harry usually struggles to do his homework so she publicly praises him for completing it this time (even though he only answered half of the questions). | Ms H has marked a class set of homework and see them the following lesson. She says well done to those who have done their homework and gives out achievement points to students who have clearly put in more effort such as attempting the quiz more than once.<br><br>She speaks to Harry at the end of the lesson to say she has noticed he attempted the homework but that if he doesn't complete it, he won't gain the benefits. She asks him how she can help him with completing the homework, offering time at lunch that day to complete the homework. |

In which of these classrooms do you think Harry will attempt the homework in the future and consistently? My own classroom has looked like both of the scenarios above, and I can tell you with confidence that Harry would consistently attempt the homework if my classroom was more like Classroom B. In fact, when my classroom has been more like A, even more students stopped attempting their homework properly, and the norm is one of doing homework for the sake of it but without much thought or effort.

Let us unpick why that is.

In Classroom A, Harry has only completed half the homework but is praised for it despite there being students who have spent considerably more time and effort on it. These students are not singled out but are praised and rewarded as a homogenous group of students who have done their homework.

If I were one of these students, I'd feel less appreciated than Harry and come to view the homework as not worth my time. Even though doing the homework would have massive gains in terms of confidence and achievement, these are not immediately obvious.

In Classroom B, students are only rewarded if the homework they complete goes above the expectations of the class. The norm here is one of 'everyone does their homework – this is expected'. If someone puts in additional effort, they are *unexpectedly* granted a reward.

Returning to my anecdote about receiving a Staff Star on Fridays – if I received a nomination every single week, I would soon expect them, undervalue them and feel that I should be rewarded for simply doing my job.

In the same way, if our students are routinely rewarded for doing what is expected of them, any value they hold for the task will be diminished and replaced with the expectation of being rewarded becoming the norm.

### What Should Rewards for Homework Look Like?

When it comes to homework, the following would be most effective when giving rewards:

- Acknowledging homework completion – 'The majority of you have done your homework. You will start to see the benefits of this soon!'

- Recognising the effort that students have put in to their homework – To Samuel: 'I can see you attempted this question more than once to improve your answer, Samuel'. To the rest of the class: 'That is exactly the type of work ethic I expect from you all'.

- Explicitly linking homework completion to success in the classroom – 'Well done for answering that question so confidently, Josie. Your homework has clearly helped you here'.

- Giving an extrinsic reward such as an achievement point for work that goes beyond our expectations – 'I am impressed with this additional work you have done, Seema. You have clearly worked hard on revising electricity!'

## Sanctions

Sanctions refer to a set of disciplinary measures or consequences employed to address undesirable behaviours displayed by students. These actions aim to create an environment conducive to learning and instil a sense of responsibility amongst students.

The nature and extent of sanctions can vary widely amongst different schools, depending on their ethos and context. Typical sanctions for homework include written comments or detentions, either at lunchtime or after-school. Moreover, schools may also have a system of escalating sanctions, which increase in severity if undesirable behaviour continues. Alternatively, some schools have removed sanctions for homework entirely.

### So, Should We Sanction?

As Tom Bennett says in his book, a sanction should deter. It should not be extreme, inconsiderate or disproportional to the event leading to the sanction. A sanction should give the message that there are consequences for undesirable actions.

Having said that, why do students not complete their homework?

- They don't get the homework.
- They don't have the time.
- They don't have the right resources such as reliable internet connectivity.

- Their circumstances mean they are struggling with their mental health.
- They have missed a lot of the content.
- They don't think they will be successful.
- They forget to do their homework.
- They cannot be bothered.

Of all these reasons, it is only the last point that would be classed as an undesirable behaviour. For every other reason, the student either has no choice but to not do the homework or struggle to see themselves succeeding at it.

If we decide to sanction any student for an incomplete submission or lack of homework, we need to first ascertain the reason for their actions.

We can group all the reasons for a lack of homework into three categories:

| Category 1: circumstances | Category 2: lack of resources (mental and physical) | Category 3: lack of motivation or organisation |
|---|---|---|
| They don't have the time.<br><br>Their circumstances mean they are struggling with their mental health. | They don't get the homework.<br><br>They don't have the right resources such as reliable internet connectivity.<br><br>They have missed a lot of the content. | They don't think they will be successful.<br><br>They forget to do their homework.<br><br>They cannot be bothered. |

The level of support we provide depends on the category our students fall under, but it is also worth noting that students do not simply remain in one category.

*Category 1: Circumstances*

Students cannot help their circumstances and it would be unfair of us to sanction students without first understanding their situation and providing the relevant support. This is not to suggest that we cannot do anything for students whose circumstances mean they cannot do their homework. Chapter 6 explored ways the parent, school and student can work together to minimise the effects of circumstances and to allow students to have every chance of success.

In summary, providing additional support in terms of a Homework Club, drop-in sessions and regular check-ins can be beneficial to students.

*Category 2: Lack of Resources (Mental and Physical)*

If students do not have the right resources, either mental, such as sufficient knowledge, or physical, such as a device to work on, then we need to consider the support we can provide instead of giving out sanctions. Schools can work with parents to ensure students can easily access all the right resources to help them succeed with their homework.

*Category 3: Lack of Motivation or Organisation*

Sometimes, students have all the resources they would need and have time and space to work in, but they still do not complete their homework. With these students, it may be that they are not motivated to work either because they do not see themselves succeeding, or they don't value the homework as they cannot see the benefits in completing it. Or students simply do not want to spend their time doing homework and would rather do something else that they enjoy.

We have all had moments when we would rather do something else and put off a task that we know must be done but we just don't feel like doing it. This is despite the fact we know that doing that task will be ultimately rewarding. This is how I feel when weeding in the garden. It takes a lot of mental effort for me to want to go out into the garden and start weeding. I know the garden will look better once it is done. I know I will feel happier when it is done. But this is not sufficient to motivate me to want to do it. If I fail to start weeding, the only person it impacts is me (well, and my husband, whose eye twitches, and then he goes out and does it himself).

If our students do not do their homework because they simply do not want to, it has a greater impact than just on their own learning.

We have a responsibility to our students to help them learn and understand new content but also to learn how to learn.

In addition, students who don't do their homework will impact the norms within the classroom. When we don't sanction a student for failing to do their homework, after ensuring there are no barriers stopping them, we send the message that this is fine and is, in fact, allowed in this classroom. After a while, the norm shifts towards one where more students do not bother with their homework because they don't feel like it.

On the contrary, by giving a sanction, we hold our students to account and show them that we care about their learning and habit-building.

## What Makes a Good Sanction?

Sanctions should *deter* (Bennett, 2020). They may not correct undesirable behaviour or prevent it but they give the message that the behaviour being displayed is something that is not condoned.

When we have provided support, spoken to students and families and given every chance for them to succeed, we may have a few students who are not doing their homework because they don't want to. By giving a sanction to these students, the message becomes clear – if you do not do as asked, despite all the support and encouragement, there will be a consequence, just as there is one for poor behaviour in the classroom.

A good sanction for homework strikes a balance between promoting accountability and fostering an environment conducive to learning. Effective sanctions are clear, consistent and fair, ensuring that students understand the expectations placed upon them and the consequences of failing to meet these expectations. They should be educative rather than purely punitive, aiming to help students recognise the importance of homework in their academic growth, and encouraging them to develop better study habits.

Moreover, a good sanction should be proportionate to the undesirable behaviour, avoiding overly harsh penalties that might discourage or alienate students. For example, the first time a student misses a homework deadline, giving them an hour-long after-school detention is far too harsh, especially as there may have been a genuine reason for not completing the work.

On the other end of the spectrum, if a student consistently misses homework deadlines or only completes part of it each time, giving the student a written comment with no further consequence will not serve to discourage this behaviour. The student may feel that the consequence for not doing the homework is so minimal that missing the homework each time is worth it.

Therefore, when giving out a homework sanction:

- Determine the reason for the incomplete or missing homework.

- Give the sanction if all support has already been provided.

- The sanction should reflect the misbehaviour – possibly a shorter or less impactful sanction for the first time of missing homework, followed by a harsher consequence.

- A discussion about any further support that can be put into place, such as regular check-ins and reminders, face-to-face conversations with the student and parent.

## The Importance of High Expectations

High expectations play a pivotal role in fostering a culture of excellence and diligence within a school environment. When teachers set high standards, it signals to students the importance of homework as a tool for reinforcing classroom learning, promoting retrieval and practising independent study. This, in turn, encourages students to engage more deeply with their learning, encouraging a sense of responsibility and self-discipline. Over time, this culture of high expectations can contribute to improved academic outcomes across the school, as well as better preparation for the future.

If a student clearly puts in minimal effort with their homework and this is accepted by their teacher, why would they increase their effort levels for future pieces of homework?

What you permit, you promote (not my phrase but it is difficult to find its origin!).

If we permit little effort or incomplete work, we are promoting this work ethic.

Alternatively, by insisting on effortful, fully completed work, we communicate our expectation (and assurance) that students are capable of achieving a higher standard.

However, it's crucial that high expectations are coupled with adequate support and resources to ensure that all students have the opportunity to succeed. This includes providing clear instructions, timely feedback and additional help when necessary, as well as fostering a supportive learning environment that encourages questions and discussion.

High expectations should not morph into unrealistic demands, which can lead to undue stress, anxiety and a potentially negative impact on students' mental health and well-being. Striking the right balance ensures that students are challenged yet supported, promoting a positive attitude towards homework and learning.

Compare the first set of statements below:

| I expect you to complete all 50 questions. You have till next week to complete this. | I have set 20 questions of increasing challenge. Revise the content by using your exercise book first before attempting the quiz. You have till next week to complete this. |
|---|---|

In the first message to the class, the teacher is increasing the challenge by increasing the number of questions to complete. They have high expectations but by simply assigning many questions, there is a danger that some students would take a sanction over spending a long time working on them.

In the second message, there are fewer questions to complete and the teacher makes it clear that the challenge increases as the work progresses. However, to alleviate any stress, the teacher also provides an instruction about what to use to increase their chances of success.

Now, let us look at a second set of statements:

| I have set you 500 questions on the online platform. You can use your exercise book for support. Complete as many as you can. You have till next week. | I have set you 20 questions on the online platform. You can use your exercise book for support. Complete all questions. You have till next week. |
|---|---|

The first scenario isn't quite fictional. The person who set the first homework had genuine intentions – they wanted to set as many questions for revision as possible to help their students prepare well for an assessment. Unsurprisingly, the result was that some students felt compelled to complete all 500 questions and, naturally, struggled. Others didn't even bother to start working on them. None of the students were suitably prepared for the assessment.

Because there wasn't a clear expectation of *how much* was acceptable, there were no consequences either way. Those students who did attempt all the questions felt disheartened as a result.

In the second scenario, *all* students are expected to complete *all* questions. Everyone is treated equally but the expectation is reasonable (20 versus 500 questions).

Some people may question giving the exact same homework to all students in a class. After all, a class of students is not a homogenous group. However, a good way to modulate the challenge for students is to alter the support given to complete the same questions. For example, I set homework using Carousel Learning, which is an online retrieval platform that has the option of a revision mode whereby students can revise questions from a bank of flashcards before attempting the quiz and self-assessing. To support students further, I encourage them to use the flashcards until they feel confident before attempting the quiz. For students who can challenge themselves, I encourage them to go straight to the quiz to attempt it once and then use the flashcards to re-attempt the quiz to improve their score.

## The Importance of Consistency

Consistency in terms of homework in schools is indispensable in fostering a productive and fair learning environment. When homework expectations and sanctions for non-completion are applied consistently, it establishes a clear framework within which students can operate. They become aware of the standards they are expected to meet and the consequences that ensue if they fail to adhere to these standards. This clarity often leads to better time management, enhanced personal responsibility and a stronger work ethic amongst students as they learn to navigate the expectations set by their teachers.

Moreover, consistent homework promotes a culture of accountability. When students know that there are firm, fair and predictable consequences for failing to complete homework, they are more likely to prioritise their assignments.

I remember something a student said to me early in my career. I noticed that they were consistently not attempting my homework but they had never missed homework in a different subject. When I asked them why that was, they said it was because they knew they would be given detention if they missed their other homework. It made me stop and think. I genuinely believed I was consistently following the consequence system for non-completion of homework. But when I reflected on my practice a bit more closely, I realised I had been accepting a range of excuses from students and not following the consequence system properly. In fact, I was being consistently inconsistent!

Consistency in homework sanctions ensures fairness and transparency, which are critical for maintaining trust and a sense of justice within schools.

It must be so disheartening for a student, who works hard every time, to see their peers not getting a sanction or being rewarded for minimal work. Any trust they may have in the teacher, the norms, the school or the system will be diminished. If this happens often, then that trust will seriously deteriorate.

Consistency, therefore, is key and teachers who reliably reward or sanction their students set a clear standard of academic commitment.

## Chapter Summary

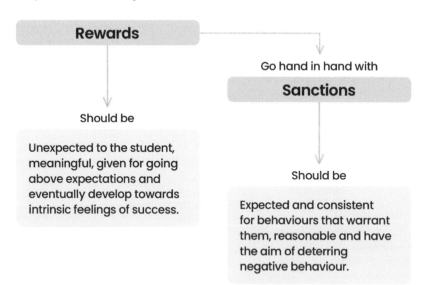

**Rewards**

Go hand in hand with

**Sanctions**

Should be

Unexpected to the student, meaningful, given for going above expectations and eventually develop towards intrinsic feelings of success.

Should be

Expected and consistent for behaviours that warrant them, reasonable and have the aim of deterring negative behaviour.

## References

Bennett, T., 2020. Rewards. In: *Running the Room*. Woodbridge: John Catt Educational Limited, pp. 269–278.

Lepper, M. R., Green, D. and Nisbett, R. E., 1973. Undermining children's intrinsic interest with extrinsic reward: A test of the "overjustification" hypothesis. *Journal of Personality and Social Psychology*, 28(1), pp. 129–137.

# 8 Building a Homework Culture

A colleague recently said to me: 'We've really thought about the home-work we set but how do we get our students to enjoy it?'

This is not quite the right question to ask. When we set homework, we expect our students to think hard, organise themselves and persist when coming across something challenging. The enjoyment usually comes once a person can see that the effort they have put in reaps them rewards. But even then, a person may not feel enjoyment, they may however feel satisfaction or a sense of accomplishment.

So instead of focusing on getting students to enjoy homework, we need a culture where doing homework:

- is the norm
- means you succeed in building confidence, habits and attainment
- is a seamless extension of learning that need not only take place in the classroom

Entire books have been written about building a culture in schools. Our aim should be to build a culture of homework in which:

- Teachers think about what they are setting, ensuring it is based on the principles of learning.
- Teachers value the information they get from completed homework and are responsive to it.

DOI: 10.4324/9781003434986-9

- All staff value the purpose of homework and support it through their words and actions.
- Students value the homework they are receiving.
- Students put in effort and know that doing their homework benefits them.
- Parents understand the value of homework and support their child.

Therefore, a sustained homework culture is one which involves our three main stakeholders: school staff, parents and students. In Chapter 4, we have already explored how students can be motivated to do their homework and how 'doing homework is the norm'. In Chapter 5, we looked at how parents and families can be encouraged to support their child with homework.

In this chapter, I will discuss how a staff culture around homework can be developed.

Firstly, we need to look at what culture actually means.

## What Is Culture?

In her brilliant book, *School Staff Culture*, Ruth Ashbee defines culture as 'the way we do things here' and 'the way it feels to work here' (Ashbee, 2024). Ashbee warns us that culture is not policy and it cannot be controlled. However, armed with knowledge, reflection, openness and evaluation, we can build a shared understanding and *impact* culture.

So if we want to influence culture, we need to first:

- Gather as much information on homework: What makes homework effective? How is homework set in different schools? What are the principles of effective learning?
- Gather as much information on the current setting and context: How can we extend learning beyond our classrooms? What barriers might we face? How can we mitigate these barriers?
- Develop a vision, purpose and shared understanding of effective homework.

- Gather knowledge to build and sustain a homework culture: how do staff feel about setting homework? Is there an impact on workload or time when setting homework? How do students feel about completing homework? Are there any grey areas that mean culture-building is hindered?

## Vision and Purpose

In *The Power of Teams*, Sam Crome tells us that working towards a purpose is the cornerstone to building and sustaining a thriving culture (Crome, 2023).

A well-defined vision sets the tone and provides a *direction* for all stakeholders in schools to work towards. Having a clear vision and purpose provides *assurance* that everyone is aiming for the same goal. There is cohesion, echoing 'the way we do things here'.

Imagine two schools:

| School A | School B |
|---|---|
| School A has a homework policy that states that departments set homework that suits their subject matter. Students are expected to complete their homework and there are rewards for those who complete the homework and sanctions dedicated to non-completion.<br><br>Mr H in Science sets homework because he overplans his lessons and wants students to complete the work at home. Sometimes, students have only the same evening to complete it for the next day when they have their lesson. | School B has a policy that states that whilst the exact task type and frequency is determined by departments, homework must be set regularly (weekly or fortnightly) and must not take more than 30 minutes. All tasks must be linked to learning in the classroom, modelled in lessons, recognised and students and parents must be made aware of websites or books to support them. However, the expectation is that students complete the work independently. There are rewards in place for students who go above these expectations and sanctions with support and discussions for those who do not complete the work. |

(*continued*)

| School A | School B |
|---|---|
| Meanwhile, Mrs T in Spanish sets homework because the Head of Department (HoD) says they should set something each week. She sets her classes tasks and checks them in lessons but because this takes time, this only happens rigorously at the start of the year. By the middle of the year, the homework tends to be making posters or infographics that she then sticks on the wall.<br><br>In the same school, Ms P in History sets essay questions because she wants her students to practise application of knowledge. She collects them each week and marks them, giving detailed feedback to students. She is close to burnout because she is marking nearly every evening. | Mr K in geography, Mrs U in French and Ms W in religious education set a short retrieval task each week based on content their classes have covered since the start of the year. They look through the responses quickly noting the questions that students struggle on and ask similar questions in lessons after providing feedback.<br><br>Mr P in art sets short pieces of work where students have to practise a skill they have learnt in class. He provides all the materials needed and offers lunchtime and after-school time for students to complete the work independently in school. |

In School A, homework has no well-defined purpose. It is clear that homework is considered important and some thought has been given to it. Additionally, departments are given autonomy over what the homework entails, how it is set and what happens with it once submitted.

The teachers at this school set homework that suits their lessons and teaching. However, there is no shared vision or direction. The same student will be missed for not completing their homework in one lesson but get caught out in another. Over time, that student will learn to prioritise the subject where they get the most sanctions for failing to do their homework.

Even if there is a clear purpose to homework in one or a few subjects, the fact that there is no cohesion in the school means homework is viewed as something that has to be done rather than a natural extension of learning.

In School B, all teachers know exactly why homework is valued and why they must set it. The purpose also dictates the importance of format, style, regularity, access and feedback. This means no matter what subject they go to, the underlying principles for setting homework are the same and students are getting the same message everywhere.

## Shared Understanding

Once a vision and purpose is determined, the next step in establishing a successful homework culture is to ensure there is a shared understanding of *why* homework is being set and *how* this will be implemented. Every person working in the school, the students and their families need to appreciate and respect the reasoning behind setting homework.

A shared understanding comes from:

- Clear definitions of key ideas

- Knowledge of perceptions and implementation

- Openness and trust

- Appropriate actions

### *Clear Definitions of Key Ideas*

Ambiguity is the enemy of successful culture development. Take for instance the scenario below:

Farah and Kamal teach English. As per the school homework policy, they both give detentions to students who do not complete their homework by the deadline. Kamal also gives detentions to students who submit incomplete work.

In addition, Farah has a homework board where she reminds her classes of upcoming homework deadlines. Kamal's classroom does not have a homework board.

Student A is moved from Farah's class to Kamal's and now keeps getting caught out by the subtle change in expectations and lack of visual reminders.

This could have been avoided if the reasons for sanctions were clearly defined within the English team. For instance, it may be decided that detentions must be given if students submit incomplete or no homework, provided support and reminders are routinely available to students. This could be followed by examples of good and not-so-good practice so all members of the team know exactly what successful implementation of a homework policy looks like.

Well-defined key ideas ensure consistency in practices across a school. This clarity undoubtedly helps in setting expectations and standards for homework. For instance, when a school explicitly prioritises and defines homework integrity, students understand and value the importance of honesty, and teachers have a clear framework to address issues like copying answers from an online search engine.

Moreover, clearly defined key ideas empower teachers to make decisions that align with these principles. For example, the science team may explicitly discuss and determine the type of feedback given for homework. This may entail picking out common errors and misconceptions and addressing them in future lessons. The team may also decide on providing feedback no more than a week following the submission of homework. If a teacher in this team decides to provide exam questions for homework, they must carefully think about how and when they can provide feedback on it that aligns with the core tenets of effective science homework feedback. Will the length of the exam question task mean marking and providing feedback within a week will be achievable? Will students need to mark their homework answers in lessons? How will this impact lesson time for teaching?

Most importantly, clearly defined key ideas provide a foundation for assessing and improving school culture. They offer benchmarks against which the effectiveness of practices can be measured.

When it comes to homework, the following are key ideas that must be defined, discussed, refined and maintained:

- What effective and ineffective homework look like in a particular subject.

- How regularly homework should be set.

- How students are reminded about and supported to complete homework.

- How students are expected to submit homework (and find it if they misplace their own copy).

- How teachers recognise the efforts made by students.

- What (and when) sanctions and rewards are given.

- What effective and ineffective feedback for homework looks like.

- When feedback is given on homework.

- How information from homework can be used to inform future teaching and homework tasks.

In order to clearly define these key ideas, it is important to gather sufficient knowledge.

### Knowledge

Ashbee informs us that there are different types of knowledge that can influence culture (Ashbee, 2024). They can be categorised into transcending and contextual knowledge.

Whilst contextual knowledge is, as the name suggests, context specific and determined from the current setting, transcending knowledge goes beyond contexts and can be applicable in different settings.

There is also knowledge of self, which can affect our internal world or habitus.

When building a culture of homework, school leaders need to determine what general principles work regardless of context and which ones are relevant for their current context. Forming subject-specific and context-specific communities can support school leaders in gathering important knowledge.

Once the knowledge of the core aspects of a homework culture is built and developed, school leaders need to focus on knowledge of perceptions and implementation.

## Knowledge of Perceptions

Perception is how people interpret and make sense of events. It is subjective and can vary greatly from person to person. The process of forming perceptions plays a crucial role in how people interact with their surroundings, influencing their reactions, decisions and interactions with others.

In a school, staff and students form perceptions using cues and their own habitus.

For instance, a teacher who notices that policies are inconsistently followed and vaguely worded will form the perception that these are not to be strictly followed. They will start to form their own framework that may be at complete odds with the initial intention set out by the policy writer.

Or a student whose family do not value homework will perceive it to be of little importance thereby putting in minimal to no effort when completing it.

Due to the fact that perceptions depend on the individual, gathering knowledge on them is vital when building a successful culture.

## A word of warning on meaning-making

We know that 'meaning is made in the mind of the learner' (Cottingham, 2023). This is true even for school leaders and teachers as they make meaning and form perceptions to make sense of their environment. Take this scenario:

Gavin is the Deputy Headteacher in charge of homework at his school. He wants to know if everyone is setting homework regularly as that is one of the core principles they established as a school. He speaks with the HoDs individually and gathers information from them about their teams and whether there are any issues with setting homework regularly. All HoDs suggest homework is being regularly set and there are no immediate issues to address.

When taking student voice about the new structures related to homework, he identifies that students in art are getting homework but the day they are set this homework seems to change each time. A couple of students are finding this difficult to manage due to not knowing when to expect homework in art.

Gavin returns to speak to the HoD for art and finds out that even though in art, they are setting homework once every 2 weeks, the day this homework is set changes, which does mean that sometimes students have a full 2 weeks and at other times, they realistically have less time. On further discussion with the HoD for art, Gavin realises that due to the infrequency of lessons in the subject and the impact of trips, out-of-lesson activities and bank holidays/INSETs, students miss their art lessons and this affects when homework can be set. In addition, as the homework is linked to current learning (and is clearly well thought-out), if the current learning does not take place, the corresponding homework cannot be set.

There are two key misunderstandings that are revealed from this knowledge-gathering exercise:

- Homework in art is mostly based on current learning, whereas the general principles suggest homework should incorporate retrieval practice.

- Regularity of homework has been interpreted to mean approximately regular rather than on the same day following each time interval.

Gavin could therefore provide time and support to ensure the art team has the chance to reconsider what effective homework in art looks like, ensuring it incorporates more retrieval practice and does not just depend on the current learning.

Another thing Gavin and the HoD for art can do is to discuss what 'regular' means and to iron out any ambiguity related to the term. Is *approximately* regular homework acceptable? What is the reason for assigning regular homework? If it is to ensure students know exactly when to expect homework, then setting homework on the same day every fortnight is more helpful than at any point within a fortnight. However, if this is indeed the case, Gavin will need to work with the Art team to mitigate issues arising from missed lessons and lost classroom time.

## Knowledge of Implementation

Perceptions relate to how people respond to and implement a strategy. If a person values a policy and understands the reasoning behind it, they are likely to implement the policy as intended. However, sometimes, despite understanding the *why* behind a strategy, other factors may influence actual implementation. This is why it is equally important to gather knowledge of implementation.

Let us look at a scenario to illustrate this.

At Rohit's new school, a homework policy is in place where students complete short tasks each week. These tasks should be on paper as most of the students attending this school struggle with reliable Internet access. Rohit fully supports setting homework and got into a great routine at his previous school where he set it using an online platform. The platform enabled him to assess and provide feedback easily, linking the questions directly with questions asked in the lesson. Although he understands why an online platform would not work at his current school, he is struggling to set, assess and provide feedback on written pieces of homework and, as a result, the homework he does set is not regular.

Unless Rohit explicitly asks for help, school leaders may be oblivious to his struggles with setting homework and may not easily uncover the issue with irregular homework. The HoD would be the first person to gather the knowledge of how their team are coping with setting short tasks each week. These are some questions they can consider and seek answers to:

- What are the short tasks based on?

- Would a central bank of tasks support the team?

- Is weekly homework sensible considering how often the team sees their classes?

- Do all members of the team have a manageable number of classes for whom they are expected to set homework?

- If there is a member of the team with too many classes, how can the HoD support them to set and collect in homework? For instance, if some are shared classes, could the homework be shared out between the class teachers as well?

- How are staff checking and giving feedback on the short tasks?

- How do the short tasks inform future teaching?

- How do Mock exams or other events impact on homework setting and checking? Do these times during the calendar warrant an alternative approach to homework?

The answers to some of these questions may well give rise to further questions and the HoD could speak to the Senior Leadership team for support. By having an outline of whether the implementation of a policy is manageable and does not give rise to barriers, school leaders can use this information to work with staff and ensure the school is working towards the same goal.

## Openness and Trust

Openness is crucial to a successful culture. It demonstrates respect, trust and a commitment to realising a shared vision.

But whilst understanding is vital in the initial stage of building a culture of homework excellence and value, in order to sustain it, there must be trust.

Trust can take many forms:

### Between Teachers and Leaders

There must be trust between the teachers who set homework and those who lead teams within schools, expecting homework to be set. If a teacher struggles to regularly set homework due to workload or illness, it is important that this is recognised and effective support is put in place. For instance, can the HoD set retrieval tasks for the class during their main teacher's absence? Or can tasks that are time-drains be minimised or altered so homework is not one more job to implement; therefore, potentially losing its meaning and impact in the long term?

Equally, there must be trust from leaders that the teachers they lead and line manage will set effective homework without being micromanaged. Sam Crome calls this 'trustful autonomy' where staff know they are trusted to do their jobs without being checked up on constantly (Crome, 2023).

### Between Students and the Teacher

Students need to be able to trust their teachers to set homework regularly rather than sporadically and support them if they ask for help. If students feel they cannot approach their teacher about homework, they may not feel able to fix any issues they may face and so ultimately won't reap any benefits of independent study.

There are inferences teachers can make about whether students work hard during their homework by asking similar questions in the classroom but these are only proxies. Teachers should, therefore, also be able to trust that students will follow instructions and complete the tasks to the best of their ability.

## Between Teachers and Parents

From the perspective of teachers, trust is crucial as it allows them to confidently communicate their expectations and homework tasks to parents. When parents trust that teachers are designing homework aimed at improving their child, they are more likely to support and reinforce learning at home. This collaboration and cohesion not only ensures that students receive consistent messages about the importance of education but also helps identify and address any challenges early on. When trust is present, parents are more likely to engage constructively with teachers and seek guidance when unsure about how to support their child.

## Appropriate Actions

Dale Carnegie, author of *How to Win Friends and Influence People*, once said: 'Knowledge isn't power until it is applied'. School leaders can spend a great deal of time gathering knowledge about perceptions and implementation but without doing something with that knowledge, all the openness and trust that may have been built up will erode and the culture collapses. This is an ongoing process – gathering knowledge, discerning perceptions and taking appropriate actions.

School leaders can take three types of actions (Ashbee, 2024):

- Anticipatory
- Responsive
- Interactive

## Anticipatory Actions

This is a direct result of the transcending and contextual knowledge-building exercise that must take place during the early stages of the introduction of a policy.

Leaders must determine if aspects of a strategy are manageable and if there are any anticipated barriers to successful implementation. This knowledge can come from:

- Discussions with similar schools where similar strategies are already in action. For example, schools that have already focused on retrieval homework may have identified during the course of implementation that having a bank of core curriculum knowledge would have been helpful from the start.

- Discussions with middle leaders and staff who will be directly involved in implementing the strategy. For example, through discussions with HoDs, it may be identified that some subject groups would find weekly homework tasks difficult when they only see their classes once a fortnight. This would mean ensuring that the term 'regular homework' is defined clearly but not rigid such that some subject teams do not feel included.

- Discussions with families to determine if the strategy can be successful. For example, if some students find it difficult to complete homework at home due to other commitments, identifying and understanding these followed by putting appropriate support in place will enable these students to be included in the homework strategy.

### Responsive Actions

These actions arise from knowledge gathered once a policy has been implemented. Leaders can seek feedback through a number of ways:

- Discussions with middle leaders and teachers: these can be part of line management meetings and scheduled into the calendar.

- Staff voice: these should be calendared. However, there should also be opportunities for staff to voice their opinions or concerns on matters whenever needed, with no risk of judgement.

- Drop-ins: this can be in the form of learning walks or simply catching up with staff.

- Data: leaders can look for trends in homework sanctions and rewards and seek to understand these by discussing them with the relevant staff.

- Student voice: giving students an opportunity to describe their views on homework strategies can be useful in understanding the impact of the culture that is being cultivated. Whilst student viewpoints can provide valuable detail about the participant perspective of a policy, leaders must bear in mind that students have varying backgrounds and habitus that can influence their perceptions. They will also have varying levels of maturity and may be swayed by populist ideas and opinions.

Leaders can use information from these different sources to build a picture of the school culture and take appropriate action.

For example, if data suggests that a particular class is receiving a large number of homework sanctions in one classroom compared to another (perhaps comprising some of the same students in a different subject), then leaders can seek to understand the reasons behind this. It may be revealed that the teacher of that class is following the policy exactly whereas the other class teachers are not responding to missed homework. In this case, leaders can determine the barriers faced by the other class teachers and work with them to develop a shared understanding of why and when to use sanctions.

## Interactive Actions

In *School Staff Culture,* Ashbee describes the various approaches to interactions that leaders can take in order to develop a sustainable culture. The following approaches relate to developing a homework culture.

- Visibility, presence and warmth: a leader who is more present and warm in their interactions develops psychological safety and trust in their colleagues. This allows staff to feel they are able to take concerns or suggestions knowing they will be heard and acknowledged.

- Modelling behaviours and sharing experiences: equally, leaders who share their own experiences and model positive homework-setting and checking behaviours open the conversations that are vital to seeking knowledge. Staff will be more likely to share their own experiences openly. Additionally, the modelling will reduce the highly negative viewpoint of 'us versus them' when it comes to staff and the leadership team.

- Removing threats: the biggest barrier to openness is a lack of trust due to perceived threats. If teachers feel threatened when they are approached by leaders, they will find it difficult to seek support, relate concerns or share opinions truthfully.

- Avoiding judgementalism: when staff struggle to share the same viewpoints, it can be easy to be judgmental through our actions and facial expressions. We know that to make homework effective, it takes a lot of effort and thought. It is unhelpful to be judgemental or even to *appear* judgemental when aiming to get all staff aligned in their thoughts and actions in developing a homework culture.

- Open-to-learning conversations: instead of skirting around an issue (termed a soft-sell approach) or being rigid in your approach (hard-sell), having open-to-learning conversations means leaders are seeking to understand viewpoints, identify causes for misunderstanding and finding a way forward that values all stakeholders. For instance:

> *Hilda, the Geography HoD, has identified that one of her team, Xizhi, is setting* homework *regularly but is not feeding back on it as often. This has come to light through student voice and lesson drop-ins. Hilda speaks to Xizhi.*

> **Hilda:** 'Some of the students I spoke to have suggested they only receive feedback from their homework once in a while. Is that your viewpoint as well?'

> **Xizhi:** 'Yes, I am finding it difficult to provide feed back every time because I have so many other things to do like planning and I am not prioritising homework feedback'.

Instead of:

**Hilda:** 'Planning is important, so if you can try to give more home-work feedback that would be great but if not, I understand'.

Or:

**Hilda:** 'I understand you are busy but the policy says we must provide feedback on each piece of homework so this is what I expect to see from now on'.

An open-to-learning conversation would look something like this:

**Hilda:** 'Feeding back on homework is important as students will start to value it less over time without it. However, as you rightly say, planning is key too. Shall we look at how we can minimise some of the other jobs you have to do so we can ensure you have time to plan and feedback on homework effectively? Perhaps, collaborative planning and shared resources may help?'

## A Note on Habits

Habits are important. They help us mitigate the limitations of our working memory and increase efficiency when performing tasks. A habit of setting homework on the same day each week for a class means we are less likely to forget weeks into the term.

But habits can be good or bad. If a teacher gets into the habit of setting homework but never checking it, then students will pick up on this and not bother completing the homework they set. They may feel like they are following the school policy but there is no value in it and whatever nascent culture is being developed, will crumble.

School leaders must consider habits and how these can impact responses to changes in a school system. As with any routine, it is important to share the reasoning, demonstrate the actions needed, have simple cues to initiate the routine and incorporate practice.

The following are questions that leaders can reflect on to help them support staff with building effective habits on homework setting and checking:

- What cues can staff use to help them follow the core principles of an effective homework culture?
- What cues can be made obvious so staff remember to set and collect in homework regularly?
- How can the act of setting homework be made simple, straightforward and, therefore, routinised?
- How will staff provide feedback so that it doesn't significantly impact lesson learning time or their own workload?
- Are there clear examples of when to give sanctions or rewards for homework?
- How can assigning a sanction or reward be made straightforward?
- Are there shared resources that can be developed to support staff?

## Chapter Summary

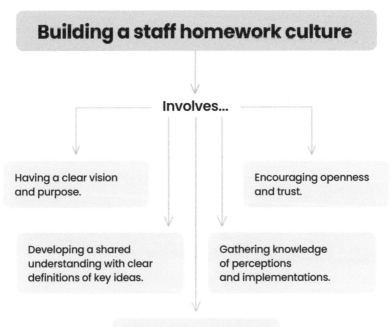

**Building a staff homework culture**

Involves...

Having a clear vision and purpose.

Encouraging openness and trust.

Developing a shared understanding with clear definitions of key ideas.

Gathering knowledge of perceptions and implementations.

Acting on knowledge through anticipation, responsiveness and interactions.

# References

Ashbee, R., 2024. *School Staff Culture: Knowledge-Building, Reflection and Action*. Routledge.

Cottingham, S., 2023. *Ausubel's Meaningful Learning in Action*. John Catt Educational Ltd.

Crome, S., 2023. *The Power of Teams*. John Catt.

# 9 Examples

In this chapter, you will find examples of the following to help you develop a homework culture at your school:

- Core principles

- Staff Continuing Professional Development (CPD)

- Communication with parents

- Assembly structure

- Department-specific policy

- Effective homework

## Core Principles

These are the principles that can form the foundation of a homework culture within a school. The following is an example of core principles that can be used to build a homework culture (Figure 9.1).

The lowest layer of bricks represents the basis of the homework strategy – homework is set regularly and appropriate support is given to students.

The next layer of bricks represents the actual type of homework – in this case, homework must be spaced retrieval practice.

DOI: 10.4324/9781003434986-10

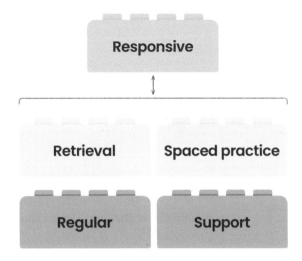

*Figure 9.1* The building blocks of homework.

The top layer of bricks is what teachers need to do with the information gathered from the homework submissions and how that will then inform future homework tasks.

### Clear Definitions

As we have seen in Chapter 8, a diagram alone is insufficient as there can be many interpretations of each aspect.

Here is an example of how one such term, *support*, can be clearly defined:

Support is defined as providing students with every opportunity at succeeding at the homework task. *Table 9.1* details some examples and non-examples of effective support:

Working on these definitions takes time and is a collaborative, dynamic process. Leaders should involve staff in generating examples and non-examples and determining the boundaries of the definitions. How much deviation from the examples and definition is allowed before the principle loses its impact? Does any deviation augment the principle and should therefore be included in the definition?

| *Table 9.1* Examples and non-examples of supportive homework practices. | | | |
|---|---|---|---|
| **Example** | **Why is this an example?** | **Non-example** | **Why is this a non-example?** |
| Providing worked examples of the task so students can refer to these whilst attempting the homework. | A worked example shows and reminds students of the steps they need to follow to achieve success. | Providing an answer sheet to all the questions. | An answer sheet means some students will simply copy these out and not spend any time thinking about the answers. |
| Providing numbered steps for instructions or a checklist, including the approximate time that must be spent on the homework. | This gives students an idea of how long they need to put aside for the task and helps them with managing their completion of the task. | Providing a number of tasks with no breakdown of what the steps are or how much time must be spent. | Students will feel overwhelmed with the task and may struggle to manage the completion of all parts of the task. |
| Practice of using an online platform in the classroom. | Students can feel empowered to use the online platform and can iron out any issues with logging on or finding the assigned task. | Assigning an online piece of work with a help guide to guide students to use the platform. | A help guide seems useful in practice but on its own can distract from the main point of the task. Students may spend too long working out how to use the online platform with the help of the guide than on the task itself. |

## Staff CPD

For all staff to convey the same message and to feel part of the culture being cultivated, homework should form part of the CPD provision. Initially, there needs to be a whole-school approach to share the general principles guiding homework practice. Following that, subject teams need time to discuss and develop their own homework policies that are aligned with the school's approach.

Here is an example of a general outline of CPD sessions that the whole school can participate in:

Introduce the subject by stating that learning is an ongoing process, which includes forgetting.

Cite the following pieces of research with a short description of their findings and the implications for homework practice:

- *Impact of homework on attainment* (Cooper, 2006; EEF, 2021).

- *Importance of spaced retrieval practice* (Furst, 2022).

- *Desirable difficulties and their role in learning over time* (Bjork, 2020).

- *How can homework develop self-regulation* (Zimmerman, 2005)?

Explain that homework only works if it has certain attributes.

Introduce the general principles for effective homework practice.

Provide staff with a description of each principle, with definitions, examples and non-examples. Provide time for staff to read, digest and reflect on these. Ask staff to start thinking about these principles when setting and collecting homework.

After a suitable period of time allowing staff time to read through the definitions, send out a survey asking for any principles staff feel need to be added or altered. Gather knowledge on reflections following sharing of the principles.

Modify the principles as needed.

Speak to Heads of Departments to further gather knowledge on how subjects may view the principles differently and identify similarities across the school. Speak to support staff to gather views from their perspective.

Collect student voice to determine their perceptions of homework.

In a future session, return to the principles with scenarios to test the boundaries of each principle. Ask the subject groups to reflect on these. Share the outcomes of the survey, student voice and discussions.

Give time to staff in subsequent CPD sessions to further develop their homework practice individually and in subject teams as part of their discussions on curriculum and classroom teaching.

## Communication with Parents

Once the general principles and foundations of a homework policy are decided on, sharing and explaining the purpose of homework with parents should come next. It is important that when a homework culture is being built and prior to sharing information on the general principles with students, parents and carers are fully informed and on-board. This is because when homework is spoken about with students, they are hearing the same message from all parties.

Communicating with parents should take a number of different routes so all parents feel included:

- A letter outlining the key principles that homework at the school will follow and how staff will support students.

- A video with the same information as the letter, but one that parents can return to and easily access.

- Information on the school website.

- An information event in school whilst also broadcasting live via a platform such as Teams or Zoom so parents who cannot attend can participate.

These forms of communication are crucial so as many parents as possible can be included. However, the message around homework needs to permeate other communication about learning. Any newsletters sent out can routinely include information about homework or explicit examples of how students have succeeded with their classwork due to the homework they are completing and *vice versa*. Below are examples of a letter sent out initially, at the start of an academic year and a section of a newsletter featuring homework:

Dear Parents and Guardians,

As we begin a new academic year at Castelino School, we wish to extend a warm welcome to you and your children. We think carefully about the education we provide your children from the lessons they are part of to the extra-curricular opportunities to help them on their way to becoming confident and responsible people.

Homework plays a crucial role in reinforcing and extending the learning that occurs in the classroom. We want to share with you our homework principles and expectations that inform our work within the classroom.

### Routine
Homework will be set on a regular basis and this will be communicated with your children regularly. The consistency and familiarity that routine homework brings will help students develop a disciplined approach to their studies and enable them to manage their time effectively.

### Spaced Retrieval Practice
This term refers to a learning technique where students review information they've learned over time. Instead of cramming, students

revisit key concepts regularly, which helps transfer this knowledge into long-term memory. For example, a topic covered in class may be revisited in homework assignments a few days later, then a week later, and so on. This method has been proven to greatly enhance memory retention and understanding.

**Support for Homework**
Our teachers are dedicated to providing the appropriate support needed for students to complete their homework effectively. This includes clear instructions, resources, feedback, and additional help where necessary. We encourage students to approach their teachers if they find any aspect of their homework challenging.

**Responsiveness**
Teachers will use homework not only as a tool for practice but also as a way to gauge student understanding. The responses from homework will inform teachers about areas that might require more attention in class. Furthermore, homework will be thoughtfully designed to align with what is being taught in class, ensuring that it is relevant and effective.

Our main aim when setting and responding to homework is to help your children to succeed: in their confidence, in their habit-building and in their academic attainment.

All we ask is that you support your children by positively encouraging them, ensuring they have the space and time to complete homework and by communicating with us if there are any barriers so we can support them to succeed. Homework is most effective when children think about the task and work on it independently. It is then that they can reap the many benefits of completing homework.

We look forward to a productive and successful year ahead and thank you for your continued support and cooperation.

Sincerely,
Headteacher
Castelino School

An excerpt from a school newsletter sent out mid-way through the academic year:

> It was great to see so many of our students thinking hard in lessons. Mr Hunter's Year 9 class were hard at work on algebra and it was great to hear them talk about how the homework that week helped them remember key concepts needed for the lesson.
>
> In Mrs Gautam's lesson on forces, students struggled with resultant forces so I saw excellent modelling in response and a careful consideration of the questions her Year 10s were asked to complete at home.
>
> A reminder that homework club runs every day at lunchtime and after school in the Study Room.

## Assembly Structure

Homework is most impactful when students fully understand why they are being set it and that it is worth effort and time on their part. Assemblies are part of the dissemination of information to students.

Here is an example of the first assembly explaining the importance of why homework is set. The descriptions are what the person giving the assembly might say as images representing these are displayed.

> Slide 1: Daisy is learning about the structures of animal and plant cells in lessons. She had an argument with her best friend at break and so she is struggling to focus.
> Slide 2: Daisy's teacher uses mini-whiteboards a lot so she does manage to listen and answer the questions in the lesson.
> Slide 3: Three days go by before Daisy has another Science lesson. The teacher asks questions about cell structure but Daisy can only remember the nucleus. The teacher goes through the structures again and starts talking about bacteria and specialised cells. Daisy is starting to feel confused.

Slide 4: A week passes by and it is Science again. Daisy cannot remember most of the structures and is feeling lost in the lesson. She cannot answer any questions confidently. She decides to day dream instead.

Slide 5: What could Daisy have done differently? She could have controlled how she was feeling in the lesson when she had an argument with her friend. She could have paid more attention to the lesson. She could have asked for help.

Slide 6: But there are many things that affect how much we listen and think in lessons.

Slide 7: Forgetting is a natural process and important for long-term learning. Every time we learn something, forget it, recall it again, forget it again and then recall it again, we make sure that memory gets stronger over time. So if you learn something on Day 1, the forgetting-retrieval cycle can help you remember that something better for your assessment on Day 30 and for your GCSEs on Day 578.

Slide 8: Daisy's teacher could help with this forgetting-retrieval cycle by setting homework. If the homework had questions on cell structure as well as other questions a few days after they are first taught and then in some of the tasks set over the following weeks, Daisy would forget and retrieve this knowledge a few times.

Slide 9: At Castelino School, we think carefully about what learning must take place for you to succeed. When I say succeed, I mean get more confident, manage your time well, be organised and build good study habits, do better in your assessment and feel motivated.

Slide 10: To help you with these goals, we set homework regularly, we make sure the tasks focus on helping you remember important knowledge long-term, we support you by ensuring you know exactly how to do your homework and succeed and we give you feedback to help you improve.

Slide 11: We also use the information from your homework to help us teach you in lessons to narrow any gaps and give you homework that will truly help. We don't just set really easy or very hard homework.

Slide 12: What can you do? Do your best when you do your homework, ask for help when you need it, use the homework to develop your long-term learning so you can succeed.

Following this first introductory assembly, which can be given to students following the initial staff CPD and parental communication, a further assembly later in the year might include useful information for students who struggle with homework. The structure below outlines what could constitute such an assembly:

*Prior to the assembly, gather knowledge from teachers, support staff and students to find out what barriers students face when completing homework, what students in similar situations do to complete homework and how teachers help students specifically.*

Slide 1: We set homework to help you learn better. The work you do in the classroom informs the homework and the homework you do informs work done in the classroom.

Slide 2: Homework helps you feel more confident, feel successful in your lessons and improve your study habits. It also helps you do well in assessments.

Slide 3: But sometimes, it can be difficult to find the time or to focus at home or to answer questions when you missed the lessons when that content was taught. We want you to know that we are here to help. First, let us see how you can help yourself.

Slide 4: Max is a student in Year 9. He has football training 3 times a week and plays matches during the weekend. He is also learning to play the guitar and has to practise this at home. Max still does his homework on time and tries his best. Here is how he does it.

Slide 5: (either a video clip or Max speaking) I have a calendar at home in my bedroom and I plan when I am going to complete different pieces of homework. It helps that my teachers set homework on the same day each time so I know when to expect it. For example, my Science teacher sets us a Carousel homework every Wednesday. I know how to use Carousel Learning and so I can revise the questions using the flashcards first and then try the quiz. Sometimes, if I have any more time and I know I have a Science test coming up, I redo the homework during the week. If I get homework that I don't understand or that will take me longer than I expect, I speak to the teacher before the deadline and ask for help. For example, my Geography teacher lets me come in at lunchtime to complete the homework in his classroom so I can ask for help if I need to.

Slide 6: Thank you, Max. Here is another student who tries their best with their homework. Sylvia forgets to write in her homework in her planner properly. She also loses sheets and gets distracted when it is an online homework. Here is how she has improved with her homework.

Slide 7: I was getting a lot of homework detentions because I kept forgetting my homework. I don't get as many these days. I spoke to the Head of Year and now we have a board in each classroom where the homework and date it is due is written. My teachers remind me to look at the board and my form tutor does too. I also do my homework in school when I can, after school so I don't have to worry about it when I get home.

Slide 8: Thank you Sylvia. Here are some suggestions that you can follow if you struggle with homework.

Slide 9: If you feel you don't have much time because of extracurricular activities or helping with younger siblings: speak to your teachers and Head of Year, try to complete homework here at school during lunch or after school, create a plan so you know when you get time to do independent study, ask your teachers to help you with making this plan and stick to it.

Slide 10: If you feel you don't get the homework: speak to your teachers who have set the homework, ask for support and resources that you can use. Maybe a website you can visit or a textbook you can use. Spend time looking at these in school if you can and ask for help if you are not sure about it.

Slide 11: If you feel you are not motivated to do your homework: speak to your teachers and Head of Year. Talk about why you are not motivated and what your goal is when it comes to school. Doing your homework will help you get more confident with your learning and do well. It will help you when it is time to revise for exams and in the future.

Slide 12: If you struggle with organising yourself such as by losing worksheets or forgetting to do your homework: speak to your teachers and form tutor. Make a plan that you share with them and make sure you have a place you can look if you misplace sheets.

Slide 13: Together, we can work towards helping you succeed. Take control of your learning by asking for help if you need it and thinking about your learning through homework.

## Department-Specific Policy

A whole school policy with general principles and definitions is useful as a foundation for each subject team to build on. The exact form that homework takes may be different in different subjects. Leaders must recognise that having the exact same structure and style to seek consistency will remove the effectiveness of the homework task, minimising any benefit to learning.

But some consistency is useful to ensure students are getting the same message when it comes to homework. How is this balance achieved? Here is an example department homework policy that attempts to achieve this balance between consistency and subject autonomy.

### *Homework in Geography*

**Purpose**: To enable students to develop a strong foundational knowledge of key geographical concepts.

**Regularity**: Once a fortnight at KS3 and once a week at KS4. Homework tasks should take no more than 20 minutes at KS3, 30 minutes in Year 10 and 40 minutes in Year 11.

**Types of homework**: A knowledge quiz of 10 questions where students use self-quizzing followed by one further task either online on Seneca or as a worksheet.

**How the homework we set follows the homework principles**: Questions for the knowledge quiz are selected carefully based on student work in the classroom. Students are asked similar questions in lessons to check they are following the self-quizzing technique properly. Teachers can set some questions more often if students need more practice on them. This shows responsiveness and incorporates spaced retrieval practice.

The second task is selected carefully to either push students to apply their knowledge or to further practice foundation knowledge. Teachers model how to complete this task in lessons so students feel supported and empowered to successfully complete it.

## Effective Homework

Below are a few examples of homework in two different subjects with commentary on what makes them effective and what could be improved, if anything.

### *Biology*

Students have previously learnt about cell structures and basic organisation in organisms. They are currently working on gas exchange systems.

Let's look at this piece of homework closely (Figure 9.2):

**Instructions could be more detailed but these may be routine by this point.**

**Questions start as straight-forward recall and build in complexity.**

*Answer the following questions:*

1. Draw and label a typical plant cell.

2. Where does gas exchange occur in mammals?

3. Why do oranisms need exchange surfaces?

4. Through which body structure does air first enter in humans?

5. List the four structures that the air flows into after passing through the nasal cavity.

6. What role do goblet cells play in the trachea?

7. How do single-celled organisms and small multicellular organisms typically move essential molecules?

8. Describe the sequence of events that occurs during inhalation, including the actions of the intercostal muscles and diaphram.

9. How does the process of expiration differ from inspiration in terms of the ribcage movement and the diaphragm's position?

10. Describe and explain four adaptions of alveoli in mammals.

11. Explain how the structure of a leaf contriutes to gas exchange, including terms such as stomata and guard cells.

12. Compare and contrast gas exchange in mammals and fish, explaining how each system is adapted to its environment.

**Has this been modelled?**

**This is a challenging application question. Has this type of question been modelled? Is the foundational knowledge secure?**

*Figure 9.2* An example biology homework.

Other questions to consider:

- How long are students expected to spend on this piece of homework?

- Where are students writing their answers?

- Has marking and checking time been considered when setting this piece of homework?

- How regularly do students receive this type of homework?

## *Art*

Now let us explore a piece of homework from a completely different subject – art. In this example, shared by Stephanie Dearnley, Subject Progress Leader and Art teacher at Trinity Academy Cathedral, Wakefield, art lessons take place once a week and students are given a short piece of homework every lesson. Homework is timetabled so that the tasks are clearly linked to the lesson that the homework is set in. If a lesson is missed, the homework schedule shifts so that the piece of homework that is set is still linked to the lesson in which it is assigned.

In this example, the task consists of academic text followed by questions to answer on the sheet (Figure 9.3).

Questions to consider:

- How long are students expected to spend on this piece of homework?

- Do the questions link to any retrieval questions posed in the lesson?

- Are any questions ever from previously learnt material to incorporate spaced retrieval?

- How is the homework checked?

## *Geography*

With the advent of a number of platforms, some of which are based on the principle of retrieval practice, here is an example of an online piece of homework.

Providing the reading material avoids students looking it up on websites that may not be appropriate for the task.

*Year 7 homework: Equipment research*

## Paintbrushes

Though quite different from the paint brushes used today, the first paint brushes were invented by the ancient Egyptians. A paint brush is a tool used to apply paint or sometimes ink. Paint brushes are available in various sizes, shapes, and materials. Thicker/larger brushes are used for colouring large areas and thinner ones are used for details.

Traditionally, paint brushes were made with animal hair, such as wolf, sheep and pony hair. Over time, these have been developed to become more functional and to improve how long they last. Materials such as nylon and polyester are the most common materials that you will now find brushes made out of. This improves how flexible they are and makes them easier to paint with creating smooth, neat lines.

**Points to consider:**

• What were paint brushes originally made from?
• What medium would you use with a paintbrush?
• Do they come in specific shapes and sizes?

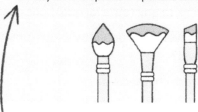

Bullet points guide the student to find relevant information before answering questions.

*Figure 9.3* Shared with permission from Stephanie Dearnley. *(Continued)*

Straightforward questions
to elicit the relevant information
from the text.

*Year 7 homework: Equipment research*

## Paintbrushes

You may need to re-visit the information on the other page.

**Questions to answer, in full sentences:**

**1. What is a paintbrush?**

A paintbrush is...

_____

**2. What did paint brushes used to be made out of?**

Paint brushed used to be made out of...

_____

**3. What medium would you use with a paintbrush?**

You would use...

_____

**4. Do they come in different sizes or one for all?**

Paint brushes come in...

_____

**5. Can you recall when you have used a paint brush?
What was it used for? What task? What medium?**

I have used...

_____

Sentence starters provided to help
students write in full sentences.

*Figure 9.3 (Continued)*

Fifteen questions are set on Carousel Learning, which is a platform where users can assign questions from a core knowledge question bank.

Students have the opportunity to study the questions in advance in the form of flashcards. In this example, the students have learnt four flashcards, got one wrong (and therefore still needs to learn it) and have 10 flashcards still to go through (Figure 9.4).

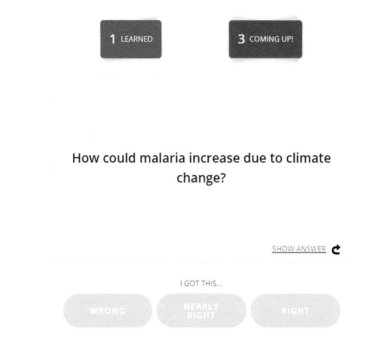

*Figure 9.4* Responsive flashcards.

Following an assessment in the form of self-quizzing, students then attempt the questions (Figure 9.5).

Finally, students can self-assess their responses against the correct answers as shown here (Figure 9.6).

To increase the effectiveness of the homework and to make the link to classroom learning more explicit, some of the questions assigned for

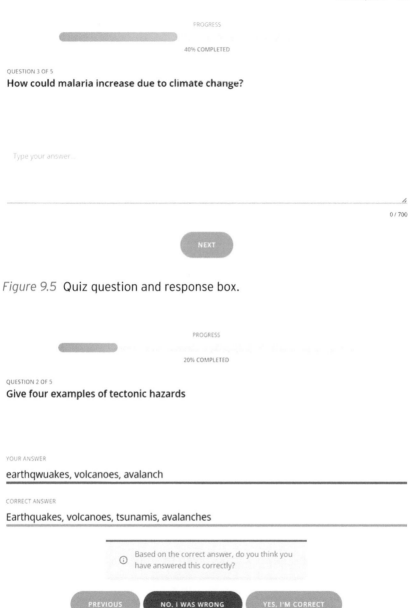

PROGRESS

40% COMPLETED

QUESTION 3 OF 5

**How could malaria increase due to climate change?**

Type your answer...

0 / 700

NEXT

*Figure 9.5* Quiz question and response box.

PROGRESS

20% COMPLETED

QUESTION 2 OF 5

**Give four examples of tectonic hazards**

YOUR ANSWER

earthqwuakes, volcanoes, avalanch

CORRECT ANSWER

Earthquakes, volcanoes, tsunamis, avalanches

ⓘ Based on the correct answer, do you think you
have answered this correctly?

PREVIOUS        NO, I WAS WRONG        YES, I'M CORRECT

*Figure 9.6* Self-assessment of answered quiz questions.

## Whiteboard Quiz - Fri 9 Feb 2024

1. Give an effect of droughts
   **Water shortage**

2. What is an ecosystem?
   **An area with biotic components and abiotic components**

3. What are the two main types of natural hazard?
   **Tectonic and climatic**

4. Give an example of a producer
   **Plants**

5. What is meant by "hazard risk"?
   **The chance of a natural hazard affecting people**

6. How could malaria increase due to climate change?
   **As temperatures increase and areas become more humid, mosquitos can spread to more areas**

*Figure 9.7* Whiteboard quiz.

homework can also be displayed on the board for a quiz that students do at some point in the lesson (Figure 9.7).

In this example, a couple of the questions in the Whiteboard quiz were also in the homework.

Questions to consider:

- How are students who do not have internet access being included when setting online homework?

- Do the question banks used on Carousel Learning cover the whole range of topics?

- Are any other homework tasks given to students with secure knowledge?

# References

Bjork, R. A. and Bjork, E. L., 2020. Desirable difficulties in theory and practice. *Journal of Applied Research in Memory and Cognition*, 9(4), pp. 475–479.

Cooper, H., Robinson, J. C. and Patall, E. A., 2006. Does homework improve academic achievement? A synthesis of research, 1987-2003. *Review of Educational Research*, 76(1), pp. 1–62.

EEF, 2021. *Homework*. (Online) Available at: https://educationendowment foundation.org.uk/education-evidence/teaching-learning-toolkit/homework# nav-closing-the-disadvantage-gap

Furst, E., 2022. *Learning in the brain*. (Online) Available at: https://sites.google. com/view/efratfurst/learning-in-the-brain?pli=1 (Accessed 31 July 2023).

Zimmerman, B. J. and Kitsantas, A. 2005. Homework practices and academic achievement: The mediating role of self-efficacy and perceived responsibility beliefs. *Contemporary Educational Psychology*, 30(4), pp. 397–417.

# 10 Frequently Asked Questions

## How Do I Get a Staff Member to Set Homework Regularly?

Teachers work incredibly hard. If they are not setting regular homework, it could be one of many reasons:

- Their workload means they struggle to do so.
- Something in their personal lives, e.g., health may be affecting their work.
- They do not believe in the homework being set.
- They do not agree with the homework policy.
- They feel that sanctions and/or rewards cause more work so don't see the point in setting homework in the first place.

Leaders need to speak openly to staff to determine their views on homework in general and specifically at the school. If it is a workload issue, look for solutions together with that staff member who mean they can set effective homework. This may mean removing something in their practice that is a time drain.

If their personal lives mean they are struggling to set and collect in homework or think carefully about the tasks, then support them with this by including their input as well as the Head of Departments (HoDs).

DOI: 10.4324/9781003434986-11

In some cases, setting centralised retrieval tasks may be the best option. Students will still get routine homework and the pressure of having to design effective tasks is minimised for the teacher.

If the staff member does not agree with setting homework or disagrees with the policy, hold an open conversation with them to understand their views and to relate the reasoning behind why homework needs to be set. Support them by explicitly showing them that the homework policy is not designed to simply give students more work but to train them in becoming independent learners.

Review how students are held accountable for poor homework completion and how this supports the students to improve their habits and the teacher in feeling motivated to give sanctions. If staff are expected to sanction, follow up on poor homework and run detentions, then over time, this can be exhausting and demotivating. Centrally run detentions within subject teams or whole school give the message that homework completion is important for the school and not just for the teacher. The message to the teacher is that the school is behind them in letting the student know that homework is important and not doing homework properly results in a sanction regardless of the teacher or subject or class.

## One of My Students Is a Young Carer. How Can I Support Them With Homework?

If the reason a student is not doing their homework is something out of their control and their parents/carers are unable to support them, then it is important to help these students to complete shorter, manageable tasks within the school day, either before or after the school day whilst in the building, or during travel periods. For example, instead of setting an essay, give them plenty of practice of this in lessons along with the rest of the class and set them retrieval questions they can do instead.

In exceptional circumstances, for instance, a family member's decline in health, it goes without saying that the student must be exempt from completing homework.

Homework is about long-term learning. It isn't about completing work for the sake of it or for an assessment. Homework should help students build lifelong habits of self-study and focus.

## I've Tried to Support and Encourage My Students but They Are Still Not Doing Their Homework. How can I Get Them to Complete Their Homework?

Sometimes we have a student who is simply not motivated and repeatedly tells us they don't need our subject. Nine times out of 10 the student does not feel belonging in the lesson. This is despite all the hard work we have put into our lessons, ensuring all students can succeed.

In these cases, it can feel disheartening and dispiriting and, therefore, easy to give up and focus on the students will do their homework. However, when we build a culture of homework, having students who openly do not do their homework due to simply 'not wanting to' could undermine everything you are trying to embed and build. Other students will slowly follow suit and find sanctions unfair when Tommy gets a pass each time because he makes it difficult for the teacher.

For students like Tommy, bring in parents/carers and have an open discussion with them as well as Tommy. Explain why learning is important, how the school helps students learn and succeed and what the school's expectations are around learning. Then outline how the homework extends the learning process and helps students with regular forgetting and retrieval. Listen to their views and determine the barriers. Most often, when I've had frank conversations like these, the student admits they don't know enough due to missing several lessons and then finds the homework inaccessible, more so than the rest of the class. Giving them a basic retrieval task focused on limited core knowledge that they can master will help them build their confidence and feel less isolated in their learning. In addition, supporting them to complete the work in a quiet space at home or school, in agreement with parents/carers, provides the student with structure and enables them to succeed in completing the task.

But these are solutions once a lack of motivation is embedded. When students are struggling with school for any reason, it is important to identify this as soon as possible and support them in the form of discussions and manageable tasks completed under supervision. Homework can help prevent the gap between these students and their peers widening over time.

## The Parents of a Child Are Not Supportive. How Do We Get Them Onboard?

This can be tricky but as we've seen in Chapter 5, it is crucial to have the same message of the importance of homework being delivered by teachers, support staff *and* adults at home. Leaders must acknowledge that parents may have differing viewpoints, in some cases bringing in their own experiences to shape their feelings towards homework.

Working with parents to understand their experiences and viewpoints is key. A powerful way to help parents see the benefits of homework is to include them in discussions of the learning process and how the school aims to support their child. Provide examples of how the homework links to the learning in the classroom and how doing the homework means their child will be less likely to forget in the long term. Present case studies of students who find doing their homework helps them gain confidence in lessons.

This is best done when other parents are present as well, in the form of an information event. It also gives them a chance to discuss potential barriers such as after-school activities that may impact on time or unreliable home internet access that means online homework may not work. Doing this at the start of the academic year is important as parents have a chance to plan how they can support their child with homework. Without this, schools will be reacting to barriers that students may face with homework later in the year and parents will not feel involved in the process.

## How Can We Avoid Cheating in Homework?

With the advent of Artificial Intelligence-driven systems (AI), such as Chat-GPT, some people are worried about students using them to help with their homework. However, cheating, when it comes to homework, is not new.

I vividly recall my classmates asking to see my answers to the homework on our way to school (yes, I did give them my answers but they still got caught out because the teacher could tell they wrote the answers on their lap on a moving bus).

On the face of it, using AI systems to generate answers to homework questions may seem impossible to detect. Even tools designed to tell us who has used AI and who hasn't are not accurate enough to confidently declare a student has cheated. There are too many false positives and false negatives to rely on these tools.

If homework is designed with learning in the classroom in mind and through the lens of a long-term learning process, then there is a way to quickly determine which students are doing their homework properly and which ones are cheating. The occurrence of cheating may be minimised with a consistent homework culture built on integrity and respect. Conversely, students are more likely to cheat in a homework culture where students know they will be sanctioned despite any barriers or where there are inconsistencies in how homework is implemented or checked. If a student is struggling, a strong homework culture may mean they seek support rather than resort to copying their answers from someone to avoid a sanction.

If you suspect a student has cheated, ask a couple of the same questions from the homework the next time you teach them in your classroom. Using a whole-class questioning technique such as mini-whiteboards means you can check if all students can answer these questions and particularly look out for the responses of the students who may have cheated.

Have a one-to-one, honest conversation with any student who you think may be cheating is the next step. Speak to them to find out *if* they have been cheating and, if they are honest, discuss why. Depending on their response, determine their barrier to completing homework well and find solutions to help them make better decisions.

In some cases, despite these discussions and support, students may still resort to cheating simply because it may be easier than actually doing the homework. Make consequences for these actions clear to students so they understand that their own learning is negatively affected by cheating.

## Should We Accept the Inevitability of Students Using ChatGPT/AI Systems and, Therefore, Encourage Their Use for Homework?

The answer to this question depends entirely on the homework task itself and the purpose of the homework.

If the aim of the homework is for retrieval of knowledge and long-term learning, then encouraging the use of AI systems directly will be detrimental to this aim. Some people suggest that AI systems can help students process their ideas into well-written text. The very act of writing, however, can help students process, improve or even generate new ideas.

As with other resources, such as search engines (some of which now also incorporate AI), we can certainly train students to use AI systems as a supplementary resource. For instance, they could be used to provide an outline for a task, to generate ideas or to explain a tricky concept in simple terms. However, it is equally important to train students in verifying information provided by AI systems, just as it has been when students use Wikipedia. This is particularly important as the work generated by AI systems appears trustworthy but can be unreliable. Explain the importance of effort, integrity and the negative impact of plagiarism to students so they know where the school stands with the use of AI in completing independent work.

## How Do We Make Sure Students Are Putting in Effort Whilst Doing Homework?

One benefit of homework is that students continue with the learning process away from your direct influence so they can build good independent study habits. However, an obvious disadvantage is that you cannot make sure they are focused and thinking about the homework whilst completing it.

The first step to ensuring students are putting in effort is to show them *how* the homework will help them with their learning. A clear breakdown of each step of the homework process and its link to the student's success could be illuminating such as the one shown in Table 10.1.

*Table 10.1* Explicitly linking steps involved in successful homework to improvement with learning.

| Part of the homework | How does this help with learning? |
|---|---|
| Working in a quiet environment | Noise can be distracting. This includes music and background television sounds. When you work in a quiet environment, your brain can focus its attention on the task instead of anything else that may be going on. This means you can gain the most benefit from the homework. Even a short period of time in a quiet environment doing your homework can help you more than working for hours in a noisy environment. |
| Answering questions from memory | The best way to help you remember core knowledge and feel more confident is if you answer questions from memory. If you simply copy down answers without thinking about it, the time you spend on homework will have little benefit to your learning. |
| | The act of forgetting and retrieving knowledge from your memory makes the connections in your memory more robust. This is exactly what you need for long-term learning. |

*(continued)*

| Table 10.1 (continued) | |
|---|---|
| **Part of the homework** | **How does this help with learning?** |
| Being persistent with the homework | A good study habit is to keep going when you face a challenging task. Your teacher will have informed you of reliable resources you can use to support you. Use these to help you instead of giving up. |
| Reviewing your answers | Before submitting your homework, it is a good idea to review your answers to make sure you have done everything in the instructions. Reviewing also means you may spot errors so you can correct them. You can be proud of the work you have put in and be content in the knowledge that the effort you have put in will benefit you. |

## Should We Pre-Plan Homework Tasks?

Pre-planned homework tasks have their advantages:

- They remove the need for designing homework tasks regularly, thereby leaving more time for planning lessons and providing feedback.

- Non-specialist teachers are supported with setting good pieces of homework.

- If a teacher is absent, homework is still set, which doesn't disrupt the homework-linked learning process.

- If all students in a year group are being given the same piece of homework, the HoD can identify common strengths and weaknesses across the cohort. This can provide valuable data to review how certain topics are taught.

However, it is important to note that pre-planning homework can remove the responsiveness that comes from designing homework with the class learning needs in mind. If the task in Week 5 is on balancing symbol equations in chemistry but your class struggles with understanding simple word equations, the homework can actually be detrimental to their learning. Indeed, in these cases, the homework becomes something to check off a list, devoid of meaning. One of the key levers of effective homework is to match the task to the domain expertise of the student.

If setting retrieval tasks, having a core question bank can be helpful. All members of the subject team select questions from this central bank but the exact questions depend on the students within their class.

If all students require the practice of specific application of knowledge, then the same task could be pre-planned and set but deviate in the form of support given to students.

In summary, ask yourself these questions:

- Do the staff in the team struggle with time in general?
- Are there certain periods of time that act as pinch points resulting in staff struggling to set effective, well-designed homework?
- Is there a significant number of non-specialists teaching a subject?
- Do circumstances mean that a member of staff would struggle to set homework regularly?
- Do the students in a year group struggle with the same concepts or retrieve the same knowledge?

If the answer is yes, then pre-planning homework tasks will likely be supportive of a consistent homework culture.

If the answer is no, then it is better to set responsive homework judged as such by the teacher of a class who is an expert in their strengths and gaps in learning.

# A Note of Thanks

So, there you have it. Homework has meant many things to many people. Some hate it with a passion, as I once did. Others see the value in carefully designed homework. Some are worried about the impact of homework on time and perceived gaps between groups of students. Others worry about the impact of a *lack* of homework on student habits, revision and attainment.

This book has the aim of bringing clarity to the homework discourse, providing a clear path for schools to make the most of the homework that is set.

Thank you for reading *The Homework Conundrum* – I hope you have found it useful.

# Index

# Did you love reading about the research on Homework?

Want to get **amazing online training for your staff** that can take their understanding even further?

**Then**

The **Teacher CPD Academy**

**is for you!**

Simply scan this QR code

Or head over to
teacherCPDacademy.com

Or email
info@innerdrive.co.uk

to request a free trial.

We **illuminate research** with **inspiring** and **interactive** modules, interviews and keynote talks.

So, do not hesitate. A **brilliant professional development platform** for all your colleagues is only a click away!